D1135305

Stores and Retail Spaces 2

The Institute of Store Planners and VM+SD Magazine's
International Store Interior Design Competition

ST PUBLICATIONS
CINCINNATI, OHIO

ISBN: 0-944094-34-1

Published by:

ST Publications, Inc.
Book Division
407 Gilbert Avenue
Cincinnati, Ohio 45202

Tel. 513-421-2050
Fax 513-421-6110

Distributed to the book and art trade in the U.S. and Canada by:

Watson-Guptill Publications
1515 Broadway
New York, NY 10036

Tel. 908-363-4511
Fax 908-363-0338

Distributed to the rest of the world by:

Hearst Books International
1350 Avenue of the Americas
New York, NY 10019

Tel. 212-261-6770
Fax 212-261-6795

Book design by Rhinoworks, Cincinnati

Printed in China

10   9   8   7   6   5   4   3   2   1

CONTENTS

EXPLORE II ISP/VM+SD STORE OF THE YEAR

Seattle
Smash Design, Seattle

Explore II features dramatic sculptural fixtures that can be seen through the store's three window walls. The fixtures and color scheme were inspired by the 1962 World's Fair, held in Seattle, as well as the "futurist" aesthetic of the 1960s and the works of modernist sculptor Alexander Calder.

Because there are no solid walls in the store, fixturing had to carry the space visually. The three window walls had to remain unobstructed, and the fourth "bubble" wall, attaching the store space to the Imax Theater, provides no wall space for merchandise display. To work around those limitations, the design team came up with a merchandising plan involving four dramatic, free-standing sculptural pieces.

A huge blue fixture in the center of the space features a large mobile balanced on top. Because of its shape, reminiscent of a trained seal balancing a circus ball on its nose, it was nicknamed "The Seal." The mobile provides constant movement in the store, drawing customers into the space.

The green "Blades" fixture provides shelving along an external wall. The backless design allows for an unobstructed view into the store, while providing a simple yet dramatic backdrop for merchandise presentation. Two other fixtures, the yellow "Sail" and the orange "Whale," occupy floor space along the third glass wall and the bubble wall of the theater.

The flooring was originally specified as slate tile, but the designers opted to go with a custom terrazzo tile in keeping with the retro feel of the store. The white marble matrix was infused with colored glass chips keyed to the fixture palette.

The fixtures themselves, designed to look like plate steel, were actually constructed of half-inch medium density fiberboard (MDF) with steel mending plates and shelf supports. Gloss enamel paint colored to relate to the sixties and the neighboring amusement park was applied by hand to accomplish the desired finish.

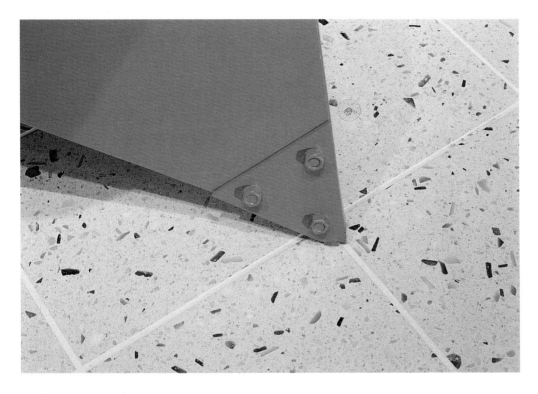

Design: Smash Design, Seattle — Harper Welch and Marc Clements, senior designers; Darrick Borowski, project designer
Pacific Science Center Team, Seattle — Carole Grisham, associate director, cfo of enterprise division; Nadine Yamasaki, store manager; Kay Wilson, finance and planning coordinator
Architect: Smash Design, Seattle (store); Denis Laming, Paris (building); Callison Architecture, Seattle (project)
Lighting Design Consultant: Denise Fong, Candela Lighting, Seattle
General Contractor: Smash Design, Seattle
Fixturing: Smash Design, Seattle
Flooring: Rover Marble and Technology, Italy
Furniture: Smash Design, Seattle
Graphics: Smash Design, Seattle
Cash Desk Tile: FritzTile, Dallas
Red Column Tile: Dal-Tile Corp., Dallas

EL PALACIO DE HIERRO

Mexico City
Pavlik Design Team, Ft. Lauderdale, Fla.

El Palacio de Hierro, looking to become the leading department store in Mexico, wanted to combine state-of-the-art planning and merchandising concepts with Old World elegance. Pavlik Design Team created a three-level vertical plaza, "The Plaza Atrium," as the store's focal point. Vistas, boulevards and galleries in textured surfaces, soft-hued colors and rich wood finishes extend in all directions. The juniors department features vaulted ceilings and ash walls and floors that provide a neutral backdrop for colorful fashions. Fine Jewelry offers a sense of privacy and exclusivity with its sable-toned wood, river-rose marble floors and sapphire area carpet. The Home Gallery uses a series of lighted arcades to display glass, crystal and other home merchandise while anigre walls and floors in blush satin and white provide warmth and understated elegance for Designer and Exclusive Fashions. This customer-conscious layout also includes toys, with colorful play zones radiating from an animated clock tower and "El Mundo Joven," a high-energy environment featuring trend-setting fashion and music for young shoppers.

Design: Pavlik Design Team, Ft. Lauderdale, Fla. — Ron Pavlik, president/ceo; Luis Valladares, director of design; Luis Martin, director of production; Manuel Cordero, project manager; Fernando Castillo, Placido Herrera, project designers; Sven Pavlik, director of lighting
El Palacio de Hierro Team: Victor Messmacher, Jorge Aguirie, Patricia Gonzalez, Salvador Varela, Darwin Taxiera, Ricardo Ferrera
Architect: Sordo Madaleno Arquitectos, Mexico City
General Contractor: Constructora Riobo, Mexico City
Ceiling: Grupo de Diseño, Mexico City
Flooring: Innovative Marble & Tile, Hauppauge, N.Y.; Emser, Los Angeles; Architectural Tile & Marble, Miami; Bruce Hardwood Flooring, Ft. Lauderdale, Fla.; Design Wood Flooring, Deerfield Beach, Fla.; Buell Hardwood Floors, Dallas; Permagrain Products Inc., Newtown Square, Pa.
Laminates: Wilsonart, Temple, Texas; Formica Corp., Cincinnati; Lamin-art, Elk Grove Village, Ill.; Pionite, Auburn, Maine
Fabric and Wallcovering: Wolf-Gordon, Long Island City, N.Y.; Designtex, Plantation, Fla.; Carnegie, Rockville Centre, N.Y.; Archetonic, Yonkers, N.Y.; Scalamandre, Ronkonkoma, N.Y.; Nature by Design, Cartersville, Ga.; Christopher Norman, New York City; J.M. Lynne Co., Smithtown, N.Y.; Prime Seta, Ft. Lauderdale; MDC Wallcoverings, Elk Grove Village, Ill.; Innovations in Wallcoverings, New York City; Arton, Memphis; Majilite, Dracut, Mass.; HBF, Hickory, N.C.; Brunschwig & Fils, New York City; Sina Pearson Textiles, New York City
Wood Veneer: Ultrawood, Pompano Beach, Fla.

BLOOMINGDALE'S

Aventura Mall, Miami Beach, Fla.
Robert Young Associates, Dallas

Translucent glass walls along the south and west facades of this three-story branch store allow natural light to filter deep into the interior by day and create a glowing sculptural image by night. Inside, signature black-and-white zigzag flooring moves customers through departments divided by overscaled mirrors framed in glass mosaic tiles. In Women's Shoes, winding low walls counterbalance the more rigid placement of furniture and fixtures. An ellipse that forms Men's Fragrances visually links Fashion Accessories and Men's World with a checkerboard floor of polished granite and cleft slate emphasizing the crescent-shaped caselines in each adjacent area.

Skewed escalators rising through the center of the store and an opening in the ceiling entice shoppers to the second level, where video monitors are positioned against the store's transparent west facade. The 59th & Lex Café is an oasis of soft light, with gleaming walls of glass mosaic tiles behind more of the etched-glass exterior windows. The residential feel is continued on the third level, where housewares, the Crystal Shop and the Dining Circle are immersed in natural and dramatic lighting.

Design: Robert Young Associates, Dallas. Bloomingdale's Team: Federated Department Stores, New York City
Architect: Kohn Pederson Fox Associates P.C., New York City
General Contractor: Whiting Turner Contracting Company, Ft. Lauderdale, Fla.
Lighting Consultant: Integrated Lighting Concepts, Westlake Village, Calif.
Ceiling: USG Interiors Inc., Chicago
Flooring: Innovative Marble & Tile, Hauppauge, N.Y.; Atlas Carpets, City of Commerce, Calif.; Trinity Hardwood, Dallas; Harbinger, Atlanta
Furniture: Burnhardt, Lenoir, N.C.; Geiger-Brickel, Atlanta; HBF, Hickory, N.C.
Wallcovering: Tri-Kes, Dallas; J.M. Lynne, Smithtown, N.Y.; Anya Larkin, New York City
Fabrics: Anzea, Ft. Worth, Texas; Knoll, East Greenville, Pa.; Schumacher, Newark, Del.; Bergamo, New York City

J.B. WHITE

Augusta Mall, Augusta, Ga.
Fitzpatrick Design Group Inc., New York City

To create a flexible and cost-effective environment that is service-oriented and easy to shop, designers created an oval "coliseum" floorplan whose focal point is a 50-ft. central atrium with escalators that face customers as they enter the 160,000-sq.-ft. store. Arches of light run in succession from the atrium to create the Cosmetics and Fragrance areas. Two murals depicting images of the community and its history flank the escalators and are emphasized by a terrazzo starburst pattern in the floor of the grand space.

Store departments were given diverse themes. Intimate Apparel, which runs along a major window wall, is delicately enhanced by draperies with festoon valances and a 7-ft.-by 3-ft. chandelier in its center. The Young Men's and Juniors departments feature a "warehouse" theme with layered sheetrock over brick walls, natural concrete flooring, epoxy-painted safety striping and hard-edged details including corrugated metal, industrial lighting and related graphic images. The Children's Department features a roller coaster and a mural of active "kids play" images along a soffit on the perimeter walls. The Market Center Home Department is marked with an open ceiling and an interplay of large and small-scale geometric patterns loosely based on a Moroccan bazaar.

Design: Fitzpatrick Design Group, New York City — Jay Fitzpatrick, president/creative director; Errol Spence, vice president/project manager; James Robertson, director of color and materials; Enrique Montalvo, Steven Derwoed, project designers
Mercantile Team: Randy Burnette, senior vice president, real estate; Ron Gosses, vice president of visual merchandising; Bruce Quisno, director of store design and construction; Lori Kolthoff, manager of store design; Earl Carpenter, manager of store planning; Debbie Lane, project manager
Architect: Hixson Architects, Cincinnati
General Contractor: Orion Building Corp., Nashville
Lighting Consultant: Merchandise Lighting, Inc., Port Jervis, N.Y.
Epoxy Flooring: Torginal, New York City
Carpet: Atlas Carpet Mills, New York City; Bentley Carpet Mills, New York City; Durkan Commercial Carpets, New York City; Interface Flooring Systems Inc., New York City; Mannington Commercial Carpets; Milliken Carpet, New York City; Monterey Carpets, New York City
Ceramic Tile: American Olean, Lansdale, Pa.; Fiandre Tile, Cincinnati; Floor Gres, Mees Distribution, Cincinnati; Imagine Tile, New York City
Glass: Allstate Glass, New York City
Marble: Landis Marble, Wilmington, Del.; Innovative Marble & Tile, Hauppauge, N.Y.; Quarella, Concord, Ont.
Metal: Ardmore Textured Metals, New York City; Farboil Company, Baltimore; Flexopan, Sandy Lake, Pa.; Lyle/Carlstrom Associates Inc., Somerville, N.J.; Milgo Bufkin, Brooklyn, N.Y.; Stylmark Corp., Minneapolis
Paint: Benjamin Moore, Newark; Sherwin Williams Co., Kendallville, Ind.; Pratt & Lambert, Marysville, Calif.
Graphics: The Joan Marcus Co., New York City
Laminates: Formica Corp., Piscataway, N.J.; Lamin-art, Elk Grove Village, Ill.; Nevamar/International Paper, New York City; Pionite, New York City; Wilsonart, New York City
Rubber/Vinyl Base: Flexco, Tuscumbia, Ala.; Johnsonite, Chagrin Falls, Ohio

Sheet Vinyl: Lonseal Inc., Dover, N.J.; Roppe Corp., Fostoria, Ohio
Special Finish: Corian, Douglaston, N.Y.; Crescent Bronze Powder Co., Chicago; Formica Corp., Piscataway, N.J.; Slaj Design Inc., New York City; Symmetry Products, Lincoln, R.I.; Town & Country Floors, New York City; Walker Zanger, Sun Valley, Calif.; Wilsonart, New York City
Terrazzo: David Allen Company, Raleigh, N.C.
Vinyl Tile: Amtico, Cincinnati; Armstrong World Industries, Lancaster, Pa.; Azrock Industries, Rutherford, N.J.
Wood: Architectural Systems, New York City; Buell Hardwood Floors, New York City; Kentucky Wood Floors, Louisville, Ky.
Wallcovering: Blumenthal, Canaan, Conn.; Carnegie, New York City; Archetonic, Yonkers, N.Y.; J.M. Lynne, New York City; Innovations, New York City; Brunschwig & Fils, New York City; Gilford Inc., New York City; Maya Romanoff, New York City; Schumacher Contract, New York City; Seabrook Wallcoverings, Memphis; Silk Dynasty, New York City; Slaj Design Inc., New York City; Tandem Contract Inc., Monmouth Junction, N.J.; Wolf Gordon Inc., Long Island City, N.Y.
Fabric: Danzian Fabrics, New York City; Majilite Corp., Dracut, Mass.; Designtex, New York City

NEIMAN MARCUS

Beverly Hills, Calif.
Robert Young Associates, Dallas

The remodel of this Neiman Marcus store marks a significant change in the design direction for all its specialty department stores. Robert Young Associates updated the classic International Style design with rich textural surfaces, clear and intense colors and bold, geometric forms. Each merchandise category offers a distinctive setting created with feature lighting and unique materials including marble and glass mosaic tiles, luminescent gold-speckled, silver and platinum-leaf wallcoverings and brightly-hued waxed plaster walls.

On the main floor, a full-height half-circle wall in hand-rubbed blue waxed plaster is the centerpiece of the women's shoe salon and is balanced by an equally imposing wall in brilliant red waxed plaster at cosmetics on the opposite side. A light slot in the ceiling, in the form of a sweeping curve, reinforces the geometry of the perimeter walls. The top level of the store, housing Men's World, gains light from a wall of unscreened windows overlooking Beverly Hills and crisp, detailed fixtures, twin slabs of steel and light oak to echo the controlled geometry of the ceiling plane. The Garden Level, transformed from office and stock areas, houses the Gallerias and Mariposa Restaurant.

Design: Robert Young Associates, Dallas — Tom Herndon, president; Sherri Mitchell, project manager; Hallie Galloway, designer; Jerry Fitzpatrick, construction administration; Mike Wilkins, creative director; Tom Ryan, construction services director
Architect: AHT Architects Inc., Beverly Hills, Calif.
General Contractor: R.D. Olson, Anaheim, Calif.
Lighting Consultant: Integrated Lighting Concepts, Westlake Village, Calif.
Lighting: Prescolite, San Leandro, Calif.; Indy Lighting, Indianapolis; Baldinger, New York City
Fixturing: Columbia Showcase, Sun Valley, Calif.; Goebel Fixturing Co., Hutchinson, Minn.
Flooring: Prince Street, Cartersville, Ga.; Durkan Patterned Carpets, Dalton, Ga.; Mohawk Carpets, Atlanta; Gallerie Dhurne, San Francisco
Laminates: Wilsonart, Temple, Texas; Nevamar, Odenton, Md.
Furniture: J. Robert Scott, Los Angeles; Donghia, New York City; James Jennings, Los Angeles; Dakota Jackson, Long Island City, N.Y.
Wallcovering: SJW, Seattle; Blumenthal, Canaan, Conn.; Silk Dynasty, San Jose, Calif.; Crezana, Southampton, N.Y.
Fabric: Brunschwig & Fils, New York City; Creation Bauman, Rockville Center, N.Y.; Edelman Ltd., Hawleyville, Conn.; Knoll Textiles, New York City

MARIPOS

NORDSTROM

Seattle
Callison Architecture Inc., Seattle;
Nordstrom Store Planning, Seattle

To integrate a fresh and modern look within an 80-year-old store, the designers consolidated 380,000 square feet from three separate buildings into five floors of retail space that features wider aisles, new lighting technology, merchandise vignettes and a light color palette. Design challenges included column size, spacing and shape, smaller floor sizes and varying ceiling heights.

Large-diameter columns were used to create rooms within rooms, breaking the scale of each department. Column grids define smaller spaces within each merchandise zone and provide new methods for presentation, including a runway effect for suited forms in menswear, "aquarium walls" in kidswear, "play areas" for cosmetics and a variety of backdrops in shoes. An open-sell concept — which pulls merchandise off shelves and onto more contemporary, flexible fixtures in materials such as light cherry wood and satin-nickel finishes — has expanded to most departments including Handbags, Men's Furnishings, Women's Apparel and Kidswear. A neutral color palette creates a soothing environment, emphasizes merchandise and combines with strong accent colors to create focal points.

Design: Callison Architecture Inc., Seattle — Nathan Thomas, principal-in-charge; MJ Munsell, retail designer; Elaine Schneider, interior designer; Craig Dinkins, Steve Harmon, Peter Watson, Phillip Goodman, project managers; Chuck Weldy, specifications
Nordstrom Store Planning Team
Architect: Callison Architecture Inc., Seattle
General Contractor: Robert E. Bayley Construction Inc., Seattle
Consultants: Wiss, Janney, Elstner Associates Inc., Seattle; RSP-EOE, Seattle; Hargis Engineers Inc., Seattle; RJA, Lerch Bates North America, Seattle; Nordstrom, Seattle
Flooring: Lees Carpet, Greensboro, N.C.
Stone: Associated Imports, Atlanta
Fixturing: Fetzer's, Salt Lake City; Columbia, Sun Valley, Calif.; Pacific Coast Showcase, Puyallup, Wash.
Furniture: Kaasco, Mukulteo, Wash.; GDM, Los Angeles
Wallcovering: Innovations, New York City; Blumenthal, Long Island City, N.Y.; Evans & Brown, San Francisco
Fabric: Pollack & Associates, New York City; Steven Harsey/Orient Express, Placentia, Calif.; ArcCom, Orangeburg, N.Y.
Graphics: Messenger Sign, Seattle
Signage: Neo-Source, Denver
Audio/Video: Liebold Communications, Seattle

UPTON'S

West Boca Square, Boca Raton, Fla.
Fitzpatrick Design Group Inc., New York City

The designers were charged with expressing the less corporate, more casual culture of Boca Raton and taking the family-style department store to a new level, appealing to a wider customer base without alienating its existing shoppers. A glass and slate-tile facade, set in dramatic contrast to the satin, stainless-steel Upton's logo, supports a classical portico that breaks into the interior, becoming a vaulted, stepped ceiling in the South Beach architectural style. A "Town Square Clock" in the heart of Fashion Accessories Boulevard implements the same concept, including the kinetic excitement of neon lights and signs.

Feature areas in front of the "Boulevard" are highlighted by a breaking-wave capital, wood floors bordered by a wave pattern of mosaic tile and glass mosaics clad to round columns. Major aisles and intersections with terra cotta flooring and inlaid mosaic borders provide new areas for merchandise presentation with accessible, modern fixtures. At the end of the arcade, the Home Store uses slow-moving belt-drawn ceiling fans and turn-of-the-century style to elicit a more relaxed atmosphere for shopping.

Design: Fitzpatrick Design Group, New York City — Jay Fitzpatrick, president, creative director; Andrew McQuilkin, vice president, project designer; James Robertson, director, color, materials and flooring; Elspeth Knox, project decorator; Michael Gnecco, project manager
Upton's Team: David Dworkin, president, ceo; Tim Heard, vice president of store planning and operations; Gary Siler, vice president of stores; Kelly Plank, vice president of merchandising; Jack Bailey, director of store planning; Doug Morris, director of visual merchandising; Mike Woods, director of store development and construction; Mark Ryan, store planner
Flooring: Buell Floors, New York City; Dal-Tile, Hicksville, N.Y.; SCF Georgia, Doraville, Ga.; Innovative Marble and Tile Inc., Hauppauge, N.Y.; Roppe Rubber Corp., Deer Park, N.Y.; Shaw Contact Group, New York City
Laminates: Pionite, Maspeth, N.Y.
Special Finishes: Surrell (Formica), Piscataway, N.J.; Technolux USA, Brooklyn, N.Y.
Paint: Benjamin Moore, Newark, N.J.; Sherwin Williams, Melville, N.Y.; Pittsburgh Paints, Pittsburgh
Wallcovering: Innovations, New York City

TRISH MCEVOY LTD.

Saks Fifth Avenue, Town & Country Mall, Houston
Callison Architecture Inc., Seattle

The cosmetics company charged its design team with portraying intimacy within a warm, residential-like area. The result, an "oasis among chaos," features soft music and aromatherapy along with a materials palette that includes quarter-sliced sycamore, Italian limestone and satin-nickel metal. The "Beauty Bar," a one-on-one consultation area, and the "Glorifiers" backwall display areas are incorporated around columns that feature stone ledges, mirrored surfaces and monochromatic colors to enhance the make-up, skincare and brush lines that drive the design's understated feel.

Design:
Trish McEvoy Team: Trish McEvoy, Geri Emmett
Saks Fifth Avenue Team: Stephen Gilbert, Dale Saylor, interior designers; Jeff McCallum, lighting designer
Architecture: Callison Architecture Inc., Seattle
Lighting: CJ Lighting; Lightolier, Fall River, Mass.; Juno Lighting, Des Plaines, Ill.
Fixturing: Proco Wood Products, Osseo, Minn.
Flooring: Innovative Marble & Tile, Hauppauge, N.Y.
Furniture: Hampton Lane, Los Angeles
Laminates: Wilsonart, Temple, Texas
Signage: Saks Fifth Avenue visual merchandising
Wallcoverings: Olea Plastering
Fabric: Knoll Textiles, Greenville, Pa.
Audio/Video: Liebold Communications, Seattle

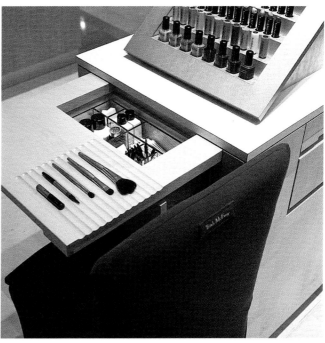

CARGO COSMETICS

Vancouver Pacific Center,
Park Royal Mall, Vancouver
MLCD Inc., Toronto

Working within a modest 250-sq.-ft. envelope, the design team was challenged to distinguish the young cosmetics company from other big-name cosmetic brands with a dramatic, convincing "first impression." Using an open plan that features a series of floating display components in maple with glass and stainless steel accents, the designers created a relaxed and easy atmosphere for "women-on-the-go." Overhead lighting, integrated with a variety of textures, gives the simplicity of the space a richness and depth, while the products, packaged in stamped aluminum tins and frosted lipstick tubes, are emphasized by focused lighting on a central tower with full-height graphics as back-drops.

Design: MLCD Inc., Toronto — Daniel Meneguzzi, design partner-in-charge; Mary Ellen Lynch, John Debortoli, Steven Comisso, production team
Cargo Cosmetics Team: Hana Zalzal, president; Barbara Alexander, creative consultant
General Contractor: Les Boiseries Plessis Ltee., Plessisville, Que.
Graphics Consultant: Joans & Morris Photo Imaging, Cargo Cosmetics, North York, Ont.
Fixturing: Les Boiseries Plessis Ltee., Plessisville, Que.
Lighting: Eurolite, Toronto
Signage: Joans & Morris Photo Imaging, Cargo Cosmetics, North York, Ont.

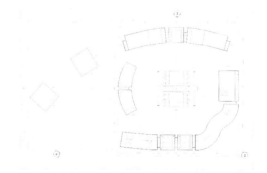

HOLT RENFREW CO. LTD.

Men's Fragrance and Intimates, Toronto
Yabu Pushelberg, Toronto

To redefine the foundation area of this cutting-edge specialty store, the design team arranged a series of niches around the perimeter of the department with two illuminated architectural columns as anchor points. The core Fragrance fixture, with an elevated base, is transparent and appears to float despite its high-capacity storage and display capabilities. The central wall fixture for Intimates provides hang-rods and glass-front drawers for display and accessible storage and features a walk-in closet as a unique "masculine refuge." A mock bathroom, complete with functioning sink and illuminated mirror, serves as the backdrop for the skin care and treatment niche. A materials palette of warm woods, textured glass and brushed steel emphasizes the wide product mix and creates a calm environment to attract the often busy, distracted male shopper.

Design: Yabu Pushelberg, Toronto — George Yabu, creative director; Glenn Pushelberg, managing partner; Polly Chan, designer; Kevin Storey, project manager; Paul Leung, architectural technologist
Holt Renfrew Team: Joel Rath, president; Jim Brandl, executive vice president and ceo; Anne Walker, vice president of construction and design; Peter Lawrence, regional manager
General Contractor: McGee Construction Ltd., Toronto
Lighting: Eurolite, Toronto; Litemore, Toronto
Fixturing: Unique Store Fixtures, Toronto
Flooring: The Sullivan Source, Toronto
Laminates: General Woods & Veneers, Toronto Fabric and Wallcovering, Perfection Rug Co., Toronto
Special Finishes: Moss + Lam, Toronto

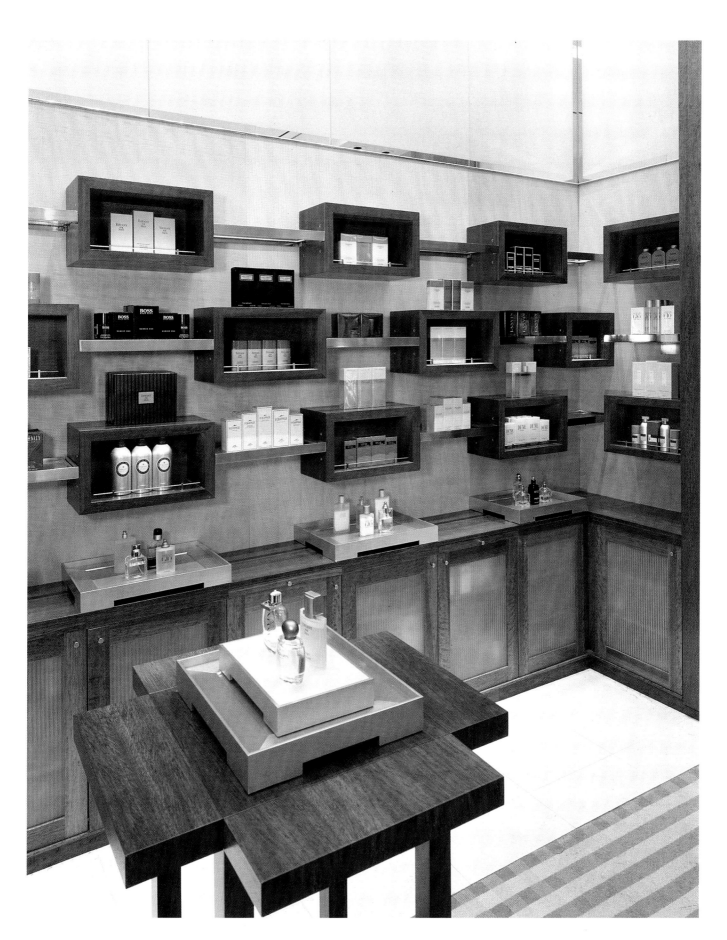

MORSE & CO.

Spanish Bay Resort, Pebble Beach, Calif.
Pebble Beach Company, Pebble Beach, Calif.
B&N Industries, San Carlos, Calif.

nspired by sweeping panoramic views of Pebble Beach's dunes, cliffs, trees and oceanfront, the focal point of this resort golf shop is a central island combining mobile display platforms, wall merchandising and shelving units that provide a variety of display opportunities. The functional, versatile fixtures in honey-maple veneers and bronze metals reflect the design team's interpretation of the surrounding environment and provide front-hang, side-hang and shelving combinations. The tie and accessory wall, featuring a series of gliding panels on concealed tracks, creates a high-impact vertical presentation using the versatile puck system that appears repeatedly in the store.

Design: B&N Industries, San Carlos, Calif. — Brad Sotiberg, president; Maureen Tollex, vice president; Max Mendez, project manager
Pebble Beach Company Team: Ken Muscutt, store planner; Kara Westcott, visual merchandising manager; Kimberly Hewett, visual merchandiser
Architect: Jeanne C. Byrne, AIA, Pacific Grove, Calif.
General Contractor: Corn Construction Co., Pacific Grove, Calif.
Lighting: Juno, Des Plaines, Iowa
Ceiling: Interfinish, Bridgeview, Ill.
Fixturing: B&N Industries, San Carlos, Calif.
Flooring: Char Fauros Tile, Salinas, Calif.
Furniture: Loewenstein Inc., Pompano Beach, Fla.
Wallcovering: Maya Romanoff Corp., Chicago
Mannequins, Forms: Almax, Toronto
Props: M. Lavine, Cold Springs, Minn.
Graphics: Cies Sexton, Denver
Signage: Instant Sign Central, Monterey, Calif.

TOTALCOM

Yorkdale Mall, Toronto
Retail Planning Associates, Columbus, Ohio

The need to educate consumers about telecom solutions for greater convenience, safety and speed, resulted in an innovative mall-based specialty store that combines Bell Mobility and Bell Canada. The store's painted-aluminum exterior provides self-help services including an electronic bill-pay dropbox and a 24-hour promotional touch-point system. Inside, reflective frosted Plexiglas on the ceiling and a full palette of blues from floor to metallic wall panels combine with maple-laminate fixtures, maple floors and neutral-textured wallcoverings to combine an aura of technological sophistication with a reassuring, residential feel.

A serpentine-suspended ceiling fixture and wood path direct clients to color-coded departments defined by lifestyle rather than brand or technology. Though on-the-floor customer service is vital to any retailer's success, customer waiting in this store is virtually eliminated through a self-service information gathering and sales process that includes several interactive touch-points, live phone-lines and video conferencing with ready-to-serve, off-site representatives.

Design: Retail Planning Associates, Columbus, Ohio — Doug Cheesman, ceo; Diane Perduk Rambo, senior vice president, creative director; Dirk Defenbaugh, account executive; Jeff McCall, strategy director; Scott Hagely, project manager; Tonya Passarelli, retail strategist; Dave Fowler, environmental designer; Bill Witherup, planner/merchandiser; Perry Kotick, lighting designer; John Hamlet, CADD technician; John Rendelman, implementation; Scott Harrison, Alan Wier, Bob Myers, Tracy Rhodehamel, Matt Reiser, new media; Steve Swing, programmer; Christian Deuber, photographer
TotalCom Team: Paul Nathaniels, director of distribution, planning & development; P. Michael Haines, manager of marketing, planning & distribution; Jim Lovie, senior vice president of sales, marketing & distribution
In-Store Interactive: Retail Planning Associates, Columbus, Ohio
Ceiling: Armstrong, Lancaster, Pa.
Flooring: Atlas Carpets, New York City
Furniture: Ula International, Toronto
Paint: Sherwin-Williams, Kendallville, Ind.
Laminates: Wilsonart, New York City
Special Finishes: Nevamar, Prosoil Distributing, St. Laurent, Que.; Alucobond, Hamilton, Ont.; Tiger Drifac, Guelph, Ont.
Wallcovering: Innovations, New York City
Vinyl Tile: PermaGrain, Media, Pa.; Amtico, Cincinnati

MILLENNIUM

Mexico City
Forma Arquitectos, Mexico City

Beyond a facade of stone and glass arches with rounded inlays of blue crystals are elements of Mexican architecture emphasized by greens, blues and reds, giving this men's multi-brand clothes and accessories store the radical change it needed to remain competitive. An acid-burned marble and pre-finished black wood floor, backlit blue glass, sloping red-inked wood ceilings and wood, metal and crystal fixtures create dimension, showmanship and emphasis.

The fitting room modules, which emerge like illuminated transparent columns, define traffic and sales areas and divide the store between "off-the-rack" and custom fit. An interior shop window of illuminated blue glass is flanked on one side by an imposing red vault that crowns the cashwrap area. Hanging aluminum light fixtures and master color lamps highlight spaces and merchandise in true color.

Design: Forma Arquitectos, Mexico City — Eduardo Avalos, co-president; Miguel de Llano, co-president; Jose Seques, chief designer
Millennium Team: Alfredo Harp Calderoni, Luis Narchi
Architect: Forma Arquitectos, Mexico City
General Contractor: Forma Arquitectos, Mexico City
Fixturing: La Madera Carpinteria, Mexico City; Ricardo de La Puente, Mexico City; Ignacio Moro, Mexico City
Flooring: Tapetes Partow, Mexico City
Furniture: Moda In Casa, Mexico City
Graphics: Laura Catalan, Mexico City
Signage: Fundicion Y Construccion, Mexico City
Mannequins: Pucci International, New York City
Paint: Panfilo Vidal, Mexico City
Limestone: Rogelio Flores, Mexico City
Photography: Jordi Farre, Mexico City

THE DUCK SHOP

Moshafsky Center, University of Oregon, Eugene, Ore.
Mobius Inc., Eugene, Ore.

This 2400-sq.-ft. shop features collegiate merchandise surrounded by a spirited display of athletic tradition from ceiling to floor, including a serpentine banner portraying the history of the University's sporting events, athletes and coaches. In the store's center, video monitors play recent sporting events and life-size graphics show off the school's most famous athletes. A curvilinear circulation path eases daily traffic flow and game-day crowds, and is supported by a rounded backwall overlaid with a large graphic of a football field. The school's team name, the "Oregon Ducks," is laser-cut on steel trim throughout the store. Laminates in green and yellow, the school's signature colors, blend with oak-veneer and brushed stainless steel fixtures to highlight merchandise. The Duck Stop Coffee Bar, located in a prominent corner window at the rear of the store, repeats the curvilinear pattern of the main shop with the use of furniture and an overhead lighting display.

Design: Mobius Inc., Eugene, Ore. — Peter Craycroft, president; Craig Wollen, design director; Sagoe Hoyle, lead designer; John-Paul Davidson, account executive; Tom Bartlett, account manager
The Duck Shop Team: Arlyn Shaufler, merchandising manager
Architect: WBGS Architects, Eugene, Ore.
General Contractor: Chambers Construction, Eugene, Ore.
Lighting: Mobius Inc., Eugene, Ore.
Ceiling: Mobius Inc., Eugene, Ore.
Fixturing: Mobius Inc., Eugene, Ore.
Flooring: Chambers Construction, Eugene, Ore.
Laminates: Chambers Construction, Eugene, Ore.
Graphics: Mobius Inc., Eugene, Ore.
Signage: Mobius Inc., Eugene, Ore.
Audio/Video: University of Oregon Bookstore, Eugene, Ore.

MOVADO

Westchester Mall, White Plains, N.Y.
James D'Auria Associates Architects, New York City

Formerly a watch company only, the client charged its design team with creating an environment that reflects its newly expanded range of products. Inspired by the company's history of quality craftsmanship, designers created an International style interior that recalls early 20th Century design from Bauhaus to early 1950s Streamline concepts.

A transparent facade prominently displays the Movado logo (originally used in the 1940s) yet blurs the line between store and mall. The plan, aligned to a single axis from front to rear, is supplemented with two "floating" island showcases that reinforce a barrier-free relationship between customer and sales person. Recessed displays along the perimeter walls feature a full range of products and shallow cantilevered showcases projected from wall panels provide intimate mini-vignettes. The rear wall uses thick glass shelves above an opal glass base to accent special accessories. Other materials include stained bird's-eye maple, custom-designed synthetic marble floors imbedded with mother-of-pearl and satin nickel-finished metal.

Design: James D'Auria Associates Architects, New York City — James D'Auria, design principal-in-charge; Douglas O. McClure, associate-in-charge; Jack Weisberg, project designer
Movado Team: Robert Donofrio, director
Architect: James D'Auria Associates Architects, New York City
General Contractor: Richter + Ratner, Maspeth, N.Y.
Lighting Consultant: Johnson Schwinghammer, New York City
Flooring: Innovative Tile & Marble, Hauppauge, N.Y.
Furniture: Houston Upholstery, Houston
Fabrics: Maharam, New York City

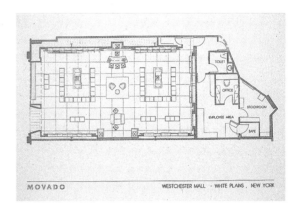

MOVADO   WESTCHESTER MALL - WHITE PLAINS , NEW YORK

REEBOK CONCEPT STORE

Suntech City Mall, Republic of Singapore
Eco-id, New York City

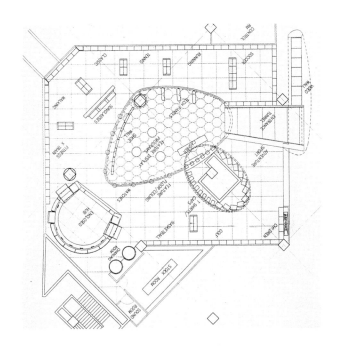

The 5500-square-foot space was designed to marry product and marketing and display the client's "technology = power" concept. The plan centers around a three-sided, egg-shaped form called the "launch pad," (a metaphor for the "flight and springiness" of its new athletic shoes) and is defined by a circular terrazzo floor pattern and a "floating" convex-shaped ceiling. Curvilinear and streamlined forms were chosen to evoke images of speed, efficiency and performance. The traditional storefront is replaced by a videowall made from 24 individual monitors that form larger-than-life images. Inside, a white palette emphasizes merchandise and creates the feel of a clean, high-tech laboratory. A gently-arched bridge of stainless steel leads the customer through a tunnel enclosed by colorful backlit graphics. In the "Shoe Wall" and "Oculus" areas, frosted plexiglass display cells and plexiglass cylinders with magnifying lenses blur the line between product and architecture.

Design: Eco-id, New York City —
Calvin Sim, Sim Boon-Yang, Peter
Tow, principals
Royal Sporting House, Singapore —
J.S. Gill
General Contractor: Woodsman
Construction, Singapore
Lighting: Kreon, Belgium
Ceiling: Formwork
Fixturing: Eco-id, New York City
Furniture: Eco-id, New York City;
Woodsman Construction, Singapore
Graphics: Work Advertising,
Singapore
Audio/Video: Sony; Bose;
Bang + Olufsen
Photography: Eco-id, New York City

EPOCA THE SHOP

Minamiaoyama, Minato-ku, Tokyo
Gunji Design, New York City

The 9800-sq.-ft., four-level shop — with two floors above ground and two floors below — is located in an upscale neighborhood in Tokyo and architecturally unified by a vertical shaft of light. The upper two floors, dressed with white encaustic-finished walls, limestone and bleached wood flooring and ebonized wood fixtures, house Better Women's Wear. Backlit false windows around an open plan balance light levels and a glass-railed staircase and inner garden provide a dramatic background to merchandise. The lower mezzanine offers a residential-styled gallery for tea and gift items, inviting customers to sit by a stainless steel fireplace or browse candles and gifts in comfort. The basement, which features cosmetics, accessories and a men's outpost, uses recessed lighting and bleached wood surfaces to brighten the windowless floor and create a welcoming open space.

Design: Gunji Design, New York City — Gunji Tachikawa, president, project and design principal
Architect: Garde U.S.P., Tokyo
General Contractor: Tansaisha Ltd., Tokyo

THE FIELD MUSEUM STORE

The Field Museum of Natural History, Chicago
Charles Sparks + Co., Westchester, Ill.

The store was designed around a graphic motif that communicates the diversity of cultures, nature and living things both past and present. The storefront is distinguished but not intrusive to the architectural character of the museum's loggia columns, high ceilings and signature off-white palette. The storefront logotype, a mosaic-tile floor design, ornamental plasterwork and large-scale custom chandeliers carry the "living things" motif throughout the store. Within the main space, a freestanding curved colonnade separates the long hall into "zones" for merchandising handicrafts from various parts of the world. Natural light was "rediscovered" from previously closed 17-ft.-tall windows. Perimeter fixtures adjacent to the windows and centrally located showcases connect customers with products. The "Kids Field Trip" area includes three-dimensional dinosaurs emerging from a fantasy jungle and a repeated jungle motif on custom-designed area rugs.

Design: Charles Sparks + Company, Westchester, Ill. — Charles Sparks, principal-in-charge, designer; Don Stone, project manager, lighting designer; Stephanie Arakowa Moore, graphic designer; Fred Wiedenbeck, color, products and materials
Field Museum Team: Laura Sadler, director of auxiliary services; Jill Mondler, merchandise manager; Chris Feine, store operations manager
Architect: Kurtz Associates, Des Plaines, Ill.
General Contractor: Pepper Construction Co., Chicago
Consultants: MEPC Engineering, Chicago
Ceiling: Formglas, Westmont, Ill.
Lighting: New Metal Crafts, Chicago
Fixturing: Midwest Woodworking, Chicago; Bernhard Woodworking, Des Plaines, Ill.
Flooring: Ann Sacks, Chicago; Brown Clay, Westchester, Ill.

LIQUOR CONTROL BOARD OF ONTARIO

Crossroads Mall, North York, Ont.
The International Design Group, Toronto

When the Liquor Control Board of Ontario (LCBO) developed the concept for a bulk-discount format store, they charged the design team to break away from the typical stark, white warehouse look and set a new standard for value shopping. The resulting design is marked by colorful bulkheads in various shapes and sizes, lower ceiling levels and distinct station finishes that reinforce specific purposes (for example the wall behind the "Cork Station" is made of cork floor tile and the "Rinse Station" features porcelain tile and MDF board). Entrance stations including "Ask Us" and "Taste" encourage immediate consumer participation under bright, suspended signage while the central attraction, the "Bottle Your Own" station, is designated by a 16-ft.-tall mural of red and white grapes that draws attention to where patrons select wines of their choice for individual bottling.

Design: The International Design Group, Toronto — Ron MacLachlan, managing director; David Newman, project manager, designer; Andrew Gallici, Ron Mazereeuw, team members
LCBO Team: Jackie Bonic
General Contractor: Rutherford Contracting, Gormley, Ont.
Graphics Consultant: Mental Art, Toronto
Lighting: Juno Lighting, Mississauga, Ont.
Fixturing: Woodart Ltd., Peterborough, Ont.
Flooring: Stone Tile International, Toronto
Laminates: Octopus Products, Toronto

THE FOOT LOCKER, KIDS FOOT LOCKER, LADY FOOT LOCKER

Arsenal Mall, Watertown, Mass.
Elkus/Manfredi Architects Ltd., Boston

This project combines Foot Locker's three brand prototypes into one triplex, allowing each to reflect the lifestyles and motivations of its individual customer types. Elkus/Manfredi Architects worked with lighting and audio-visual specialists to create the main multimedia attraction, a 24-screen videowall that creates an "urban playground" setting with images and sounds moving to satellite sets throughout the store. A fixture system of interchangeable wood, metal and glass panels incorporates sports and fashion merchandise in three distinctive environments. Specialty lighting in the men's store creates a high-impact space and displays constantly changing brand imagery while the women's shop, based on a health club and spa concept, provides a comfortable and clean environment to shop. The children's store features an oversized skateboard element, a nine-foot-diameter basketball, climbing mounds and giant closets that create a "fantasy playroom."

Design: Elkus/Manfredi Architects Ltd., Boston — David P. Manfredi AIA, principal-in-charge; Randall Stone, project manager; Andy Bennett, project architect; Jennifer Lomax, project designer; Dennis Allain, Alan Bruce, Deniz Ferendeci, Paul Karnath, Molly Nolan, Patricia Ribbeck, Tamara Roy, Frances Temple-West, project team; Bonnic McCormick, Whitney Perkins, environmental graphic designers Foot Locker Team: John DeWolf, senior vice president of real estate; John Trombley, president of store planning; Kevin Ruehle, director of store design; Melisca Klisanin, visual merchandising

General Contractor: Shawmut Design and Construction, Boston

Consultants: rh productions, New York City (show design and lighting design); Illuminart, Ypsilanti, Mich. (lighting design); Acoustic Dimensions, Dallas (audio system design); Relic, Glendale, Calif. (mural design); Scott Love Design, Milton, Mass. (interior graphics); TMP Consulting Engineers, Boston, and McNamara/Salvia, Boston (engineers)

Lighting: BASH Lighting Services, N. Bergen, N.J.; Electronic Theater Controls, Great American Market, High End Systems, Lighting and Electronics, Modular International, Special FX Lighting, Times Square Lighting, Cooper Lighting, Devon Glass, GE Lighting, Indy Lighting, Lightolier, Metalux, Lutron, Phillips Lighting, Spero

Fixturing: Ontario Store Fixtures, Weston, Ont.

Flooring: Milliken Carpet, LaGrange, Ga.; Gerbert Ltd. (Dodge-Regupol), Lancaster, Pa.

Furniture: Adesso, Boston; Montage Inc., Boston; Fondel Ltd., Lehi, Utah; Ontario Store Fixtures, Weston, Ont.

Wallcovering: Foam Technology Symmetry Products, Lincoln, R.I.

Fabric: Gilford Spectrum Vinyl, Jeffersonville, Ind.; Circle Fabrics, New York City; Annie Walwyn/Jones Ltd., New York City

Graphics: AD+, Boston; Invisuals, Boston

Audio: Acoustic Dimensions, Dallas; ECI; Signal Perfection Ltd., Columbia, Md.; Aphex Systems, Ashly Audio, Bag End, Crown International, Eastern Acoustic Works, Level Control Systems, Midiman, Tannoy

Video/Show Control: ITEC Productions, Orlando, Fla.; ITEC Productions, Alcorn McBride, Allen Bradley, American Power Conversion, Electrosonic, MAG Innovision, Netgear, Phillips, Videotek

Photography: Gary Quesada, Hedrich Blessing Photography, Chicago

COMP USA

North Michigan Avenue, Chicago
Shikatani Lacroix Design Inc., Toronto

Challenged by exterior signage restrictions and Comp USA's traditionally suburban "warehouse" look, the design team was charged with giving this new flagship store an upscale, urban look while attracting the walking or driving passerby. A three-story window provided the opportunity for an eye-catching 30x50-ft. interior logo sign, and 20-ft. tall banners and wall graphics in the lobby are visible from the street. Inside, customers take an escalator to the third-floor retail space, enjoying a 75x25-ft. "media wall" that is a collage of digital images and related audio messages. Large drywall "halos," placed to highlight each area's product and service, can be seen from any point in the store, guiding customers from one focal area to the next. Individual graphic schemes for each department are used to overpower the vibrant color palette. The "Comp Kids" theatrical area, where bright-colored tile and whimsical imagery are used to create a family appeal, revolves around a space theme, including a 13-ft. fiberglass rocket ship.

Design: Shikatani Lacroix Design Inc., Toronto — Jean Pierre Lacroix, president; Edward Shikatani, vice president, creative director; Gary Peddigrew, project manager; Eric Boulden, Kim Yokota, Jason Hemsworth, Janet Jones, Laura Shaw, Lynn Giles, Steven Comisso, Don Hood, Michelle Escobar, design team
CompUSA Team: Jim Paddock
Architect: Elkus Manfredi, Toronto
Lighting: Juno Lighting, Brampton, Ont.; Eurolite, Toronto; Lightolier, Lachine, Que.; Entertainment Technology, Toronto
Fixturing: Lozier Store Fixtures, Omaha, Neb.
Furniture: Manhattan Store Interiors, Brooklyn, N.Y.; Bonart Furniture, Newark, N.J.
Paint: Sherwin Williams, Melville, N.Y.; Benjamin Moore, Newark, N.J.
Flooring: Tarkett Commercial Floor Tile; Lees Commercial Carpet, New York City
Graphics: Collins Signs, Dothan, Ala.; Sign Graphx, Chicago

POTTERY BARN

North Michigan Avenue, Chicago
BCV Architects, San Francisco

Both challenged and blessed by the great vertical dimension of the space, the design team was charged with respecting Chicago's architectural history while expanding the client's concept into a space three times the size and two levels high. The exterior walls and columns, built of two types of limestone, recall the golden hue of the Water Tower just north of the store.

In the two-story Grand Lobby, seasonal merchandise and decorative accessories grouped around furniture provide a comfortable, fashion-oriented statement, while aisles on either side promote focused attention. Stairs lead to a mezzanine and cage elevators also move through the space. The articulation of the store allows a logical ordering of merchandise using definitive "shop" ideas. The Lighting Gallery, occupying the principal area of the mezzanine, is structured of fabricated steel, inspired both by the work of Mies Van der Rohe and the Chicago Elevated Rail Road. Opening off the Lighting Gallery, the Bed and Bath Shop hutch supports the focal wall. Anchoring the rear of the store, The Tabletop Shop employs an oversized hutch to showcase tableware and linens.

Design: BCV Architects, San Francisco — Hans Baldauf, principal-in-charge; Alessandro Latini, project architect; Richard Altuna, retail design consultant
Pottery Barn Team: Gary Friedman, president; Howard Lester, ceo; Bud Cope, vice president of store development; Thad Geldert, store design manager; Patti Kashima, store planning manager
Architect: BAR Architects, San Francisco; BCV Architects, San Francisco
General Contractor: Fisher Development Inc., San Francisco
Lighting Consultant: Ross de Alessi Lighting Design, Seattle
Ceiling: Fisher Development Inc., San Francisco
Fixturing: Environments Inc., Minnetonka, Minn.
Wallcovering: TBC Plastering, Saint Helena, Calif.
Furniture: Joe Faris Studio, Oakland, Calif.
Laminates: Environments Inc., Minnetonka, Minn.
Flooring: Mankato Stone, Mankato, Minn.
Signage: Thomas Swan Signs, San Francisco
Audio/Video: Pacific Rim Stereo, Sausalito, Calif.

THE HAGGAR CLOTHING CO. FACTORY STORE

Dallas
FRCH Design Worldwide, Cincinnati

Drawing on Haggar's more than 70-year brand heritage, FRCH Design Worldwide was charged with "putting the factory back in factory outlets" for Haggar. The store's vaulted, galvanized metal ceiling with exposed trusses, stained concrete flooring, metal shelving and old-fashioned belt-driven metal ceiling fans create a "direct-from-the-manufacturer" setting. Recycled industrial sewing machines, garment racks, shirtmaker forms, cutting tables and ironing boards also contribute to the historical/industrial mood. An exact model of the first office of company founder J. M. Haggar, Sr. was recreated on the selling floor and the "Haggar Walk of Fame" features brass inlays and personalized bricks honoring more than 220 employees who have worked for the company for more than 20 years. A mock-up of a tractor trailer used to ship Haggar's merchandise has dressing rooms hidden behind its façade.

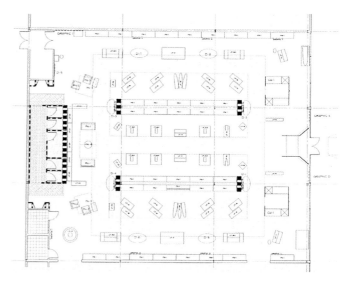

Design: FRCH Design Worldwide, Cincinnati — Kevin Roche, principal-in-charge; Chip Williamson, project architect; Amy Rink, designer; Laura Johnson, design documents; John Kennedy, graphic designer; Cynthia Turner, lighting designer; Kelly Knight, color, product and materials designer; James Frederick, merchandise presentation designer
Haggar Team: Joseph Haggar III, chairman, ceo; Frank Bracken, president, coo; Alan Burks, senior vice president of marketing; Ron Batts, vice president of retail; Bill Jasper, vice president of store operations; David Roy, vice president of technical services; Diane Gerber, director of construction; Emily Hill, director of retail merchandising; Kent Ubil, director of Haggar research; Steve Mallone, director of facilities
Lighting: Lightolier, Fall River, Mass.; Lithonia Lighting, Conyers, Ga; FD Lawrence Electric Co., Cincinnati
Ceiling: Celotex Corp., Tampa, Fla.
Fixturing: MET, Chicago
Flooring: Karastan Bigelow, Philadelphia; Crossville Ceramics, Crossville, Tenn.; Forbo Industries Inc., Hazleton, Pa.; Permagrain Products, Newtown Square, Pa.; Mannington Commercial Carpets, Calhoun, Ga.
Furniture: Beverly Furniture Mfg. Co., Pico Rivera, Calif.; Pastense, San Francisco; T.O.M.T., New York City
Fabric: Zax Inc., Denver
Laminates: Wilsonart, Temple, Texas
Paint: Sherwin Williams, Cleveland
Fiberglass Panels: Sequentia Inc., Middleburg Heights, Ohio
Door Handles: Schlage, Arlington, Texas
Grout: Bonsal Grout, Charlotte, N.C.
Signage: Victory Sign Industries, Ft. Oglethorpe, Ga.
Photography: Carolyn Brown, Dallas

DESIGNER CONNECTION

Hagertown Prime Outlets, Hagertown, Md.
Visconti Design Associates, Oakland, N.J.

At Designer Connection, which showcases current-season designer merchandise at discount prices, a two-toned color scheme of natural maple and cherry wood designates areas for women and men. Distinct presentation areas were created with merchandising bays that alternate between arched gypsum board soffits with flat-wood panels and columns with faces featuring wood panels that "float" away from the gypsum board. Lifestyle graphics, silver and gold tone Designer Connection logos and simple black-and-white logos of featured designer brands help customers chart their path through the store. Neutral carpet offsets departments while keeping the merchandise "center stage." A circular, central cash wrap with brushed-aluminum accents and an overhead fascia in natural maple and cherry anchor the gender-divided areas to the maple and cherry vinyl floor and inspire a natural traffic pattern deeper into the store and around the cash-wrap area.

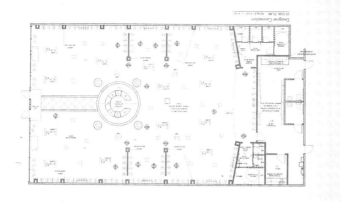

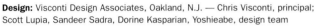

Design: Visconti Design Associates, Oakland, N.J. — Chris Visconti, principal; Scott Lupia, Sandeer Sadra, Dorine Kasparian, Yoshieabe, design team
General Contractor: David Nice Builders, Williamsburg, Va.
Fixturing: David Nice Builders, Williamsburg, Va.
Flooring: Amtico, Cincinnati
Mannequins/Forms: Grand & Benedicts, Portland, Ore.
Signage: West Coast Signs, Sarasota, Fla.
Audio/Video: Bose, New York City

EASTERN MOUNTAIN SPORTS

Commonwealth Avenue, Boston
Horst Design International, Huntington, N.Y.

I n a 100-year-old building that features dual-structural columns but no historic architectural elements, the design team chose to use one series of columns as feature wall displays and create a destinational route along the other column series. Aisle runs lead to focal walls interspersed with hanging graphics of mountain imagery and philosophical text, embodying the store's outdoor theme. The company's growing rugged footwear department was made prominent with stone columns, raw timbers and a galvanized steel display wall. Video displays, specialty fixtures and unique benches further enhance the importance of the area. A generous cashwrap and service area was created to allow maximum visibility, wide swings in seasonal traffic volumes and a customer-friendly atmosphere for consultation and product counseling.

Design: Horst Design International, Huntington, N.Y. — Douglas B. Horst, principal-in-charge; Bernhart Rumphorst, principal; Fidel Miro, planning and design director; Cynthia Davidson, director of colors and materials
EMS Team: Jennifer Meister, visual merchandising director; Brett Slane, vice president of marketing; Ron Gadhah, vice president of construction; John Neppl, senior vice president of construction and real estate
Architect: Horst Design International, Huntington, N.Y.
General Contractor: Desco Interiors, Willington, Conn.
Project Engineers: MEA Engineering, Waltham, Mass.
Lighting: Store Lighting Systems, New York City
Ceiling: Armstrong Ceilings, Lancaster, Pa.
Fixturing: Beacon Industries, Newark, N.J.
Laminates: Formica Corp., Piscataway, N.J.; Pionite, New York City
Flooring: Strizo Stone/Carpets, Carteret, N.J.; Lees Commercial Carpets, New York City
Signage: Beacon Industries, Newark, N.J.
Audio/Video: ECI, South Plainfield, N.J.

ONTARIO SERVICE CENTER

MacDonald Block, Toronto
Fiorino Design Inc., Toronto

The challenge for Fiorino Design was to accommodate different ways of providing information in the main entry area of the Ontario Service Center, a government information source used by 10,000 people each month. Designers recommended the counter location in double-volume space, promoting a stronger structural statement and ensuring visibility from above. The curvilinear approach, with a back-illuminated directory, juxtaposes the classically modern architecture of the center, while the double-sided display fixtures invite approach from a number of directions. Graphic panels explain how to use the government Internet and a freestanding signpost directs them to government departments in the complex. Visitors can access information through personal service, via the government website or through printed brochures.

Design: Fiorino Design Inc., Toronto — Nella Fiorino, principal; Vilija Gacionis, designer; Vasco Pires, Miodrag Antic, architectural technologists
General Contractor: Salwood General Contractors, Mississauga, Ont.
Graphics Consultant: Roman Milo, Toronto
Lighting: Eurolite, Toronto
Fixturing: Europtimum Display Inc., Toronto
Laminates: Nevamar, Odenton, Md.
Fabric: Maharam, Hauppauge, N.Y.
Photography: Robert Burley, Design Archive, Toronto

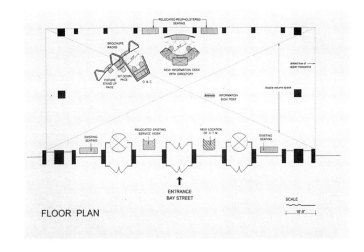

FLOOR PLAN

FOSSIL KIOSK

American Airlines Terminal, JFK International Airport, Jamaica, N.Y.
Andriopoulos Design Associates, Architects, LLC, Norwalk. Conn.

Using an early 1950s fueling station concept as inspiration, the design team captured the client's desire to mix old-time quality with the modern needs of fast-paced shopping for travel-related accessories. An internally illuminated store sign slowly rotates around the kiosk and attracts customers to the radial floor plan and central point-of-sale fixture work that allows free movement for shoppers approaching from all directions. Open metal truss work provides general illumination over merchandise displays and contrasts the interior and exterior finish materials, including flat-cut American cherry veneer, buffed natural aluminum trim and "oak" vinyl wood plank flooring. A low-voltage, overhead suspended cable system provides internal accent lighting for perimeter casework and frequently changing specialty items.

PROPOSED FOSSIL SHOP
TENANT SPACE D10
DUTY FREE INTERNATIONAL, INC.
DATE: APRIL 20, 1998

AMERICAN AIRLINES - TERMINAL NINE
DOMESTIC GATES - WEST
J.F.K. INTERNATIONAL AIRPORT
JAMAICA, NEW YORK

Design: Andriopoulos Design Associates, Architects, LLC, Norwalk, Conn., — George Newman, project team director, designer; John Marinelli, designer; Maria Genovese, technical assistant
Fossil Team: Jodi Clarke, visual merchandising
Architect: Michael Violante, Ridgefield, Conn.
General Contractor: Legacy Construction, Delaware
Engineering: ARC International Inc., Ridgefield, Conn.
Lighting: Tech Lighting, Chicago
Graphics: Empire Forester Signs, Rochester, N.Y.

LIDS KIOSK

Great Northern Mall, Cleveland
Michel Dubuc Concept, Montreal

The design team developed this 150-sq.-ft. unit using the same simple raw materials and components used in its larger stores, but added adjustable telescopic swivel mirrors, floor- to-ceiling hat walls and translucent "lid" logos to define the area as "the place to be" for the active lifestyle of Generation Y (12- to 20-year-olds). Its layout attracts cross traffic, wire-mesh fixtures maximize merchandise opportunities and fixture and lighting designs promote accessibility.

Design: Michel Dubuc Concept, Montreal — Michel Dubuc, architect, partner-in-charge; Francois Lesperance, architect, senior designer; Stephan Bernier, architect, project coordinator
LIDS Team: Bill de Vries, director of store planning; Morgan McSweeney, director of construction; John Murphy, project manager
Architect: Michel Dubuc Concept, Montreal
General Contractor: MD Collins Inc., Dearborn, Ill.
Lighting: Needham Electric Supply, Needham Heights, Mass.
Fixturing: Cabinet Systems, Largo, Fla.
Flooring: Triangle Signs Services, Baltimore
Signage: Triangle Signs Services, Baltimore
Graphics: LIDS, Westwood, Mass.

MOOZOO

Montreal
Pappas Design Studio, Montreal

Under a restricted budget, the design team was charged with developing an unconventional but dynamic science lab environment to present unique juices and chocolates made from fresh ingredients. The team focused on a playful, thematic space emphasized by vibrant-orange walls and ceilings, fluorescent-green illuminated acrylic panels and luminous trivia panels against a white background. The oval layout envelopes the customer upon entry, differentiates from the conventional straight line-up in rectangular stores and provides excess room for large line-ups at peak seasonal times. An oval cut-out ceiling, molecular-shaped lamps, acrylic domes and stainless-steel ice tables combine with economical plastic laminates, acrylic panels, paint and vinyl-composite tiles to support the modern lab theme.

Design: Pappas Design Studio, Montreal — Bess Pappas, president, designer; Susan Reed, designer
MooZoo Team: Tina Cerrao, Pino Dilloia, Anthony Dilloia
General Contractor: Construction Cama
Lighting: Juno Lighting, Des Plaines, Ill; Futura Pensieri
Fixturing: Alta Design
Flooring: Mannington Commercial Carpets, Calhoun, Ga.
Furniture: Opus; Ikea
Laminates: Formica Corp., Cincinnati; Abet Laminati, Englewood, N.J.
Wallcovering: Benjamin Moore, New York City
Signage: Bande Creative; Enseignes Paro
Props: Alu, New York City; Dalco, Hawksbury, Ont.; Cyro Industries, Rockaway, N.J.
Photography: Yves Lefebvre, Montreal

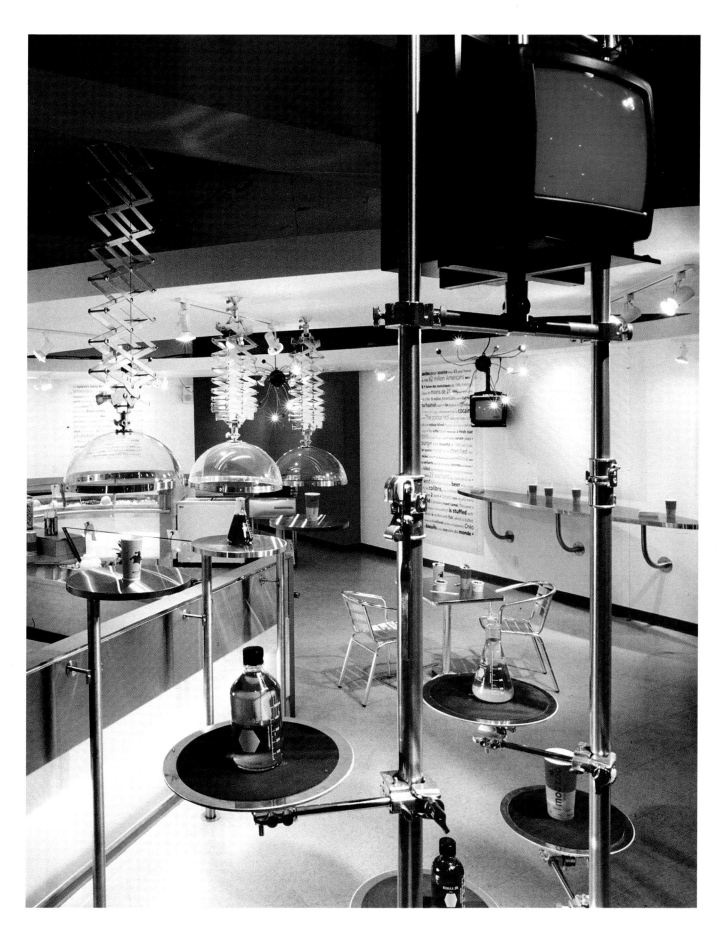

THE CHIPPERY

Vancouver
Shikatani Lacroix Design Inc., Toronto

For The Chippery's merchandise (home-made potato chips) to stand out from store-bought brand chips, the company charged its design team with creating a lively, energetic atmosphere where chips could be elevated to a new social level. From this challenge, sculptural elements, large glazing panels and colored, halo-lit channel letters with front-lit panels carved from metal tubes were created to entice customers to enter a store where imaginative graphics tell a story about the complexity of a chip's life through 12 different "chip" characters. The narrow store design, somewhat liberated by modular fixtures in maple and stainless steel, reinforces the factory-process and directs customers to the service line. The "Chip Theater" showcases chips being transported from the cooker to the 'theater,' where customers are invited to select seasonings of their choice on the fresh product.

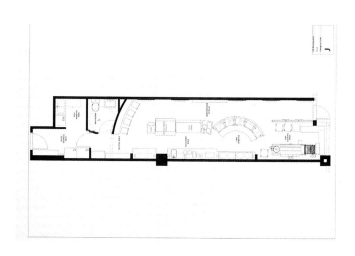

Design: Shikatani Lacroix Design Inc., Toronto — Jean Pierre Lacroix, president; Edward Shikatani, vice president, creative director; Gary Peddigrew, project manager; Eric Boulden, Kim Yokota, Laura Shaw, Michelle Escobar, design team
Fixturing: Philip Barton, Toronto
Furniture: ISA, Toronto
Flooring: DLW, Toronto; Flortech, Toronto
Wallcovering: Lescar Signs, Milton
Graphics: Shikatani Lacroix Design Inc., Toronto

MAUI TACOS

Atlanta
The Retail Group, Seattle

The design assignment for this team was to move a successful, quick-service, Hawaiian-Mex restaurant from Maui to the mainland and provide a relaxed and hip environment for customers interested in authentic-tasting food. Using a cross-cultural color palette of creams, sands and taupes combined with black, Hawaiian-style florals and lush, tropical colors, the designers used vintage photography, Hawaiian textiles and an eclectic mix of chair and table types to reinforce the comfortable, authentic feel of Maui. A salsa bar, wrapped in laminates from the chosen color palette, serves as the presentation focal point, providing on-the-spot testing and encouraging take-home merchandise opportunities that strengthen the concept that "the food is so good you'll want to take it home."

Design: The Retail Group, Seattle — J'Amy Owens, president, creative director; Cristopher Gunter, AIA, ceo; Ernie Gilbert, project manager; Greg Arhart, design director; Conrad Chin, Greg Arhart, Charlie Barttels, store planners; Ashley Bogle, Ivan Silantyev, graphic designers
General Contractor: Continental Group Inc., Cummings, Ga.
Lighting: Lighting Unlimited, Houston
Furniture: Eagle Products, Houston
Wallcovering: The Store Decor Company, Houston
Flooring: Azrock Industries, Rutherford, N.J.
Props: The Store Decor Company, Houston; Trendco, Batavia, Ohio
Signage: Bell Signs, Panama City, Fla.
Art Work: Kevin Short, Capistrano Valley, Calif.
Floor Maps: Pioneer Maps, Chattanooga, Tenn.
Menu Board: Main Street Menu Boards, Brookfield, Wis.

BRISTOL FARMS

**Kaleidoscope Entertainment Complex,
Mission Viejo, Calif.
Bristol Farms, El Segundo, Calif.**

The design objective for this supermarket was to balance historical architectural elements from the San Juan Mission with the "Old California Rancho" design of other Bristol Farms stores. Adobe facades, red-tiled roofs, earth-toned ceramic tiles and iron scrollwork are mixed with mahogany tables, floating white-glass fixtures, smoked-rust finishes and hand-patina wood trellises to bridge the gap between the two. Three large murals create focal areas in the store. In the coffee and candy area, a hand-carved foam frieze, finished to look like stone, displays the words "reap, sow, water and bountiful" to remind customers of the store's commitment to provide the finest quality products. An aged adobe wall with stone arches and black dimensional lettering defines specialty meats. Lighting racks supported by the structural framework and wall washes emphasizing fixtures for dairy and wine enhance the store's theme. Ornate iron trusses with contemporary frosted-cylinder lights, sky-blue acoustical tile panels and magenta flowers provide a colorful exit to the store.

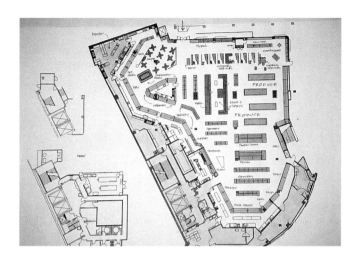

Design: Bristol Farms Store Development, El Segundo, Calif. — Debi English, vice president, head designer; Will McCoy, director of construction; Lisa Johnson, designer; Neal Aydelott, director of store planning; Cindy Doolin, purchasing manager; Suzie Kelly, construction administration
Architect: Musil Govan Azzalino, Irvine, Calif.
General Contractor: Savant Construction, Downey, Calif.
Lighting Consultant: Edward Effron, Pasadena, Calif.
Lighting: Engineered Lighting Products, El Monte, Calif.; Delray Lighting, N. Hollywood, Calif.; Lite Lab, Buffalo, N.Y.; Phillips Lighting, Somerset, N.J.
Ceiling: USG Interiors Inc., Chicago
Murals: KSM Studios, Pomona, Calif.
Wall Tile: Dal-Tile, Dallas; Tile Shop, Los Angeles
Fixturing: JF Fixtures, Long Beach, Calif.; Hare Enterprises, Long Beach, Calif.
Flooring: Morena Tile, Anaheim, Calif.; Dal-Tile, Los Angeles
Furniture: Fine Wood Finish, Huntington Beach, Calif.; West Coast Industries, San Francisco; Oasis, Malibu, Calif.; Newood Products, Eugene, Ore.
Laminates: Nevamar, Odenton, Md.
Special Finishes: Bennett & Thomas, Lagunda Beach, Calif.
Checkstands: Killion Enterprises, Vista, Calif.
Refrigerated Cases: Hussmann Refrigeration
Theming: Lexington Scenery & Props, Sun Valley, Calif.
Graphics: Maximum Visibility, Topanga, Calif.
Signage: Maximum Visibility, Topanga, Calif.
Audio/Video: DMX, Los Angeles
Photography: Bielenberg Associates, Los Angeles

CALGARY CO-OP

Hamptons Centre, Calgary, Alb.
King Design International, Eugene, Ore.

To create an upscale shopping environment with the feel of an open-air market, the design team emphasized a diagonal composition complimented by textured-ceramic wall tiles, wood-grained surfaces and outdoor plaza-like floor patterns. Major service departments, which unfold in stages to the shopper, are marked by unique tower fixtures, loosely based on the agricultural buildings and oil drilling structures that dot the Alberta landscape. Large-painted murals serve as focal points for three different departments while banners and fixture colors define and animate each space. The store's ceiling height is offset by awnings, projected bulkheads and decorative lighting. Custom-tinted corrugated metal, canvas awnings and deep paint colors enhance the environment and lend a sense of discovery.

Design: King Design International, Eugene, Ore. — William Volm, president; Christopher Studach, design director; Ira Clark, project designer; Clayton Thomson, project manager; Jessica Bell, assistant project manager
Calgary Team: Darwin Flathers, Rob Hines
Architect: Boucock Craig & Partners, Calgary, Alb.
General Contractor: Devitt & Forand Contractors Ltd., Calgary, Alb.
Fabric: Sunbrella, Glen Raven Mills Inc.
Flooring: Azrock Industries, Rutherford, N.J.
Laminates: Wilsonart, New York City

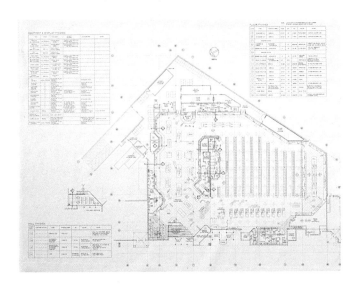

ROYAL FARMS

Baltimore, Md.
CDI Group Inc., New York City

Design: CDI Group Inc., New York City
— Gerald Lewis, principal-in-charge;
Antonio Leo, public relations director;
Kadru Yamamoto, design director;
Vlad Zadneprianski, project manager;
Nadia Zadneprianska, graphics
Royal Farms Team: John Kemp, vice
president
Architect: Donald B. Ratcliff &
Associates, Baltimore
General Contractor: Obrecht-Phoenix
Contractors Inc., Baltimore
Lighting: SPI Lighting Inc., Mequon,
Wis.; Halo Lighting, Elk Grove Village,
Ill.; Poulsen Lighting Inc.,
Ft. Lauderdale, Fla.; HessAmerica,
Shelby, N.C.; Metalux
Fixturing: Hussman; Bun-o-matic;
Falcon, St. Louis
Flooring: Crossville Ceramics,
Crossville, Tenn.; Dal-Tile, Los
Angeles; Churchville Tile
Furniture: Falcon, St. Louis
Laminates: DuPont Corian,
Wilmington, Del.
Props: Buchtail Ceramics,; Weck
Glass Block Wholesale, Crystal Lake, Ill.
Photography: Deborah Mazzoleni,
Blonkton, Md.

The design team sought to restore and enhance the original architecture of the historic building to combine Royal Farm's corporate offices and training center with a flagship store. At the entrance, custom terrazzo floors with an inlaid corporate logo project the elegance and utility of a bygone era. By exposing the barrel vault ceiling, restoring the large arched windows and creating intricate brushed-aluminum details, designers recaptured the grandeur of the "Art-Deco" theme. Modern elements are integrated with the inherent refinement of the original structure to make this a one-of-a-kind convenience store from entrance to exit.

EMPEROR'S ESSENTIALS

Las Vegas
Leclere Associates Architects P.C., New York City

Based on the era of the great Roman Empire, the design team for Emperor's Essentials, located inside the Caesar's Palace Hotel in Las Vegas, combined the looks of a Roman market place with a traditional Roman house. An overhead trellis and arched forum remind shoppers of ancient Roman architecture, while fixtures, including chariots and hanging baskets, give the feeling of a common market.

The floors are stone patterned after an ancient market place and lead the way through time. Customers are met with large delivery wagons constructed of sand-blasted ash wood with wooden wheels and black steel accessories, including a hitch at the front end. Large sculpted heads replicate the heads of common Centurion soldiers, and not the Roman gods as was traditional in Rome, because the designers wanted a common market place. Softly illuminated and standing upright on cast stone pilasters, the cast-Lucite heads add scale and detail to the architecture.

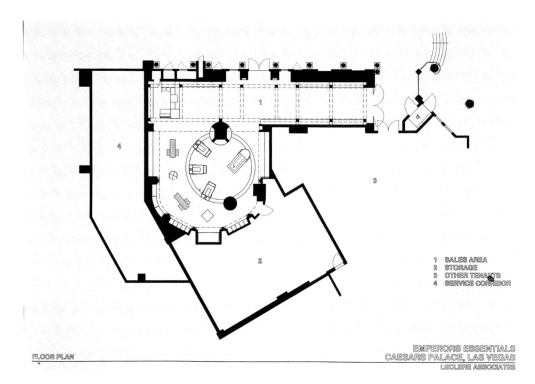

1 SALES AREA
2 STORAGE
3 OTHER TENANTS
4 SERVICE CORRIDOR

FLOOR PLAN

EMPERORS ESSENTIALS
CAESARS PALACE, LAS VEGAS
LECLERE ASSOCIATES

Design: Leclere Associates
Architects P.C., New York City —
Michael Leclere, principal; Antoinette
Torrens, designer; Craig Pillon, Woon
Lam, architects; Nikita Oak, Ella Kui,
design team
Emperor's Team: Michael Wilkins,
Mitch Simbal, Ken Farraris, Viviana
Dickieson, Laura Provenzano
Architect: Leclere Associates
Architects P.C., New York City
General Contractor: Perini Building
Company, Las Vegas
Fixturing: Dave's Custom Millwork,
Lancaster, Calif.
Laminates: Formica Corp.,
Piscataway, N.J.
Flooring: Hastings Tile, New York City
Photography: Ian Vaughan

CONVENIENCE STORE — HONORABLE MENTION

MOBIL MART

Singapore
CDI Group Inc., New York City

Sometimes the best ideas are right in front of you. That's what CDI Group, New York City, found as they drew from the company's name and based the layout of the store around the "o" in Mobil. The "o" was used as the distinguishing element that highlights the entrance, and provides an organized format for selling advertising space to manufacturers. The circular pattern encourages shoppers to continue through the store, which is kept inviting through a palette of bright reds and yellows.

This store was positioned amongst many other more mature stores. So in order to grab the customer's eye, bright, clear, and enhanced lighting combined to signal something new and different. Characterized as "funsational," the retail experience also features a new and improved foodservice program.

Design: CDI Group Inc., New York City
— Joseph Bona, president; Louis Saiz, project manager
Mobil Team: Michael Wong, retail merchandising manager
General Contractor: Kwon Ngee Eng. Pte. Ltd., Singapore
Graphics: Astro Sign Gallery, Singapore
Photography: Mobil Singapore

MARKET PLACE CAFE

CN Tower, Toronto
II by IV Design Associates Inc., Toronto

The design team and project leaders wanted the food service area of an internationally known destination site to be sophisticated but functional enough to cater to families and large tourist groups. Honeytree veneer wall panels are the backdrop for contemporary but comfortable bench seating. The elegant detail of maple, metal grid and back-lit glass fixtures at the espresso/cappuccino bar juxtaposes and enhances the elaborate cabinetry behind, in which all storage is made accessible. In the "pizza place," function and efficiency abide in butcher block stainless steel fixtures while elegance lives in the multicolored mosaic back wall. For any sized group of tourists, graceful, sturdy and lightweight aluminum armchairs are easily rearranged and generous marmoleum aisles make moving to, from, and within the dining area more efficient.

Design: II by IV Design Associates Inc., Toronto — Dan Menchions, Keith Rushbrook, Lawrence Lusthaus, Yvonne Ho, Don Collins, design team
Architect: Bregman + Hamann Architects, Toronto
General Contractor: PCL Construction, Mississauga, Ont.
Lighting: Eurolite, Toronto
Metal canopies: DNA 69
Plexiglass: Atohass Canada
Glass: CLO Glass
Base: Johnsonite, Chaprin Falls, Ohio
Cabinet pulls: Häfele America Co., Archdale, N.C.
Marmoleum: Phoenix Flooring, Phoenix
Laminates: Octopus Products
Veneers: General Woods
Butcher block: General Woods
Stone: Gem Campbell
Signage: Display Signs
Photography: David Whittaker, Toronto

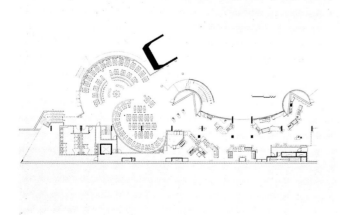

FIRE & ICE — AN IMPROVISATIONAL GRILL

Cambridge, Mass.
Prellwitz/Chilinski Associates Inc., Cambridge, Mass.

This new "improvisational grill" responds to the growing trend toward customization in retail, providing interactive and entertainment elements, as well. Customers shop from a market of fresh ingredients, which are then prepared at an 8-ft. diameter grill by staff who entertain customers while they wait.

The hot/cold theme follows through to the physical environment, which features cool-colored tumbling wall panels that lead customers from the basement entrance to the restaurant's interior. Ice dominates in the bar area, where cool blues and greens are woven into a fluid pattern of panels. Fire takes over at the grill area, where flooring and ceiling elements radiate outward like flames in shades of red, orange and gold.

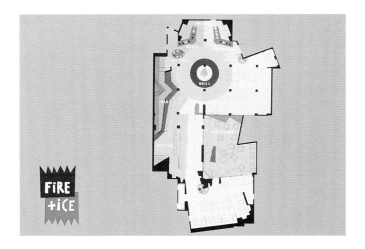

Design: Prellwitz/Chilinski Associates Inc., Cambridge, Mass. — David Chilinski, principal-in-charge; Mark Connor, project architect; Chris Brown, project designer; Susan Greco, interior designer
General Contractor: Shawmut Design and Construction, Boston
Graphic Consultants: Victoria Blanie Design, Marblehead, Mass.; Guarino Design Group, Cambridge, Mass.
Lighting: Juno Lighting, Des Plaines, Ill.; General Electric, Albany, N.Y.; Crate & Barrel, New York City
Ceilings: Addsource Fixturing: Prellwitz/Chilinski Associates (design)
Flooring: Amtico International, Shelton, Conn.; Prince Street Technologies, Cartersville, Ga. (carpeting)
Furniture: FCD (tables); Marmoleum (linoleum tops); MTS (chairs and barstools); Dodge Regupol, Lancaster, Pa. (rubber bar front); American Olean Tile Co., Sunnyvale, Texas (front of Market Station); The October Co., Easthampton, Mass. (front of Mexican Grill)
Laminates: Chemstal, East Hampton, Mass.; Gerber Limited, Lancaster, Pa.; ABET Laminati, Englewood, N.J
Paint: Benjamin Moore & Co., Newark, N.J.; Pratt and Lambert, Maysville, Calif.
Photography: Steve Rosenthal, Auburndale, Mass.

NORDSTROM CAFE

Atlanta
Engstrom Design Group, San Rafael, Calif.

The challenge facing the Engstrom Design team was to create an atmosphere that supports a restaurant concept while focusing attention on food presentation. Choosing to model the interior after a European marketplace, the team designed signage that borrows images from Renaissance-era food paintings and is framed in forged-iron art nouveau metalwork. Rich old-world details such as scalloped, solid cherry millwork, painted pressed-tin ceilings and cornices and large porcelain floor pavers form a complementary architectural backdrop in which the color and texture of food take center stage.

Soffits and ceiling coffers highlight the different areas of the restaurant, while smoothing the lines between the European marketplace theme and the modern retail environment. Modern furnishings, fabrics and lighting also blend the two themes by allowing different options for comfort and sophistication level.

Design: Engstrom Design Group, San Rafael, Calif. — Jennifer Johanson, AIA; Jeff Ellis, AIA; Nancy Kalter, AIA; Barbara Hofling, Weuli Lin
Nordstrom Team: John Clem, general manager, Nordstrom Restaurant Division
Architect: Engstrom Design Group, San Rafael, Calif.
Lighting: Electrics, San Rafael, Calif.
Ceiling: Shanker Industries, Oceanside, N.Y.
Furniture: Westin-Nielsen, St. Paul, Minn.; West Coast Industries, San Francisco
Fabrics: Justin David Textiles, El Cajon, Calif.; ArcCom, Orangeburg, N.Y.
Wallcovering: Innovations, New York City; Maya Romanoff, New York City; Marlow Brown Finishings, New York City
Flooring: Ceramic Tile Design, San Rafael, Calif.
Signage: Eclipse, Richmond, Calif.

RACE FOR ATLANTIS

Caesar's Forum Shops, Las Vegas
Bruce D. Robinson Architecture and Design, Cincinnati

To transport guests to a time and place that never was and create an exciting entry to entice prospective visitors into the ticket, preshow and main attraction areas, the design team conjured up gods, dragons, caverns and castles around a 20-foot statue of Neptune riding a sea serpent and battling a dragon. A long hall and staircase, decorated with hieroglyphics and sensual colors, leads guests to the "Main Fountain Chamber," a 50-foot high cavern where videos and graphics explain the "lost world of Atlantis." Twelve-foot-tall statues of godesses protect the "Ring of Atlantis" and guests learn through a pre-show how they can help search for the "missing ring." The "Heavens," another pre-show lead-in, features banners, flags, smoke and sparkle lights to distract visitors and guide movement to the motion-based ride on two levels. From entry to the final film itself, the sights and sounds of the Lost Continent, a world "that might have been," are inspired by the art and architecture of the world that truly was.

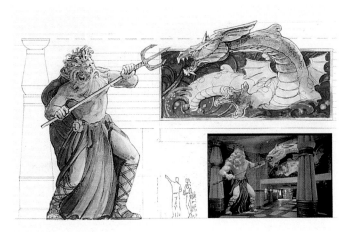

Design: Bruce D. Robinson Architecture and Design, Cincinnati — Bruce Robinson, principal-in-charge; Bruce Robinson, Mark Snell, project designers; Dan Cotton, project manager; Steve Decker, Dave Maccoy, Lucia Perani, Dave Ross, Nigel Scott, Les Schultz, Luke Stewart, Chris Wegner, design team; Jan Checo Brown, art history consultant
Idletime Network, Inc. Team: Melanie Simon, project manager; Molly Rose, project director; Bob Fleming, design director
Race For Atlantis Team: Sheryl Slakoff Inc., Las Vegas
Architect: Becket and Associates, Minneapolis
General Contractor: Ellerbe Becket Construction Services, Minneapolis
Lighting Consultant: Lightswitch
Fixturing: Nevada Discount Fixtures, Las Vegas
Flooring: Art Crete of Nevada, Las Vegas
Laminates: The Nassal Co., Orlando
Ceiling: Martin Brothers, Las Vegas
Wallcovering: The Nassal Co., Orlando
Lighting: Production Arts, New York City
Props and signage: The Nassal Co., Orlando
Audio/video: Sonics, Birmingham, Ala.
Photography: Courtesy of Bruce D. Robinson Architecture and Design, Cincinnati

CAZZIES

Columbus, Ohio
KPI Design, Columbus, Ohio

Bringing the Polynesian Islands to Ohio is no easy feat. But KPI Design jumped in with both feet. The owner of the facility wanted an outdoor enter-tainment complex, but since that was not allowed by local building codes, the design team set out to bring the outdoors, indoors.

The center piece to this large oasis is a retractable, gable skylight that brings in natural light to brighten and cheer the facility. To continue the outdoor feel, brightly colored panels float above the bar and, combined with a sculpted patterned carpet, complement and enhance the austere light of the incoming sun.

To complete the atmosphere, the bar is shaped like a peninsula, and bold French Red walls are offset by murals depicting island scenes, truly transporting customers to the islands.

Design: KPI Design, Columbus, Ohio
— Kasra Sadeghipour, project manager, planner; Craig Nowakowski, designer
Architect: David Renkes, Columbus, Ohio
General Contractor: Shahriar Kazemi, Columbus, Ohio
Photography: Courtesy of KPI Design, Columbus, Ohio

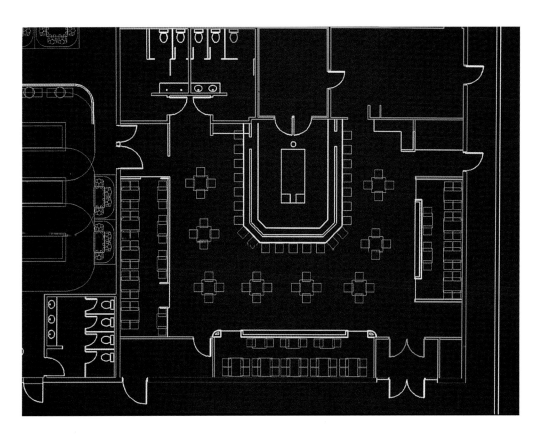

HOLLYWOOD THEATERS

Promenade Palace 12, Tulsa, Okla.
F/M Associates Inc., Dallas

s the mall movie theater a thing of the past? Not in Tulsa, Oklahoma. In fact, the Promenade Palace 12 theater has pulled the mall out of a slump, and is now competing with all of the new state-of-the-art facilities in the area. F/M Associates, a Dallas-based architectural firm, wanted an entertainment complex that would attract patrons from nearby complexes, attract film distributors and increase mall traffic in general. They did this through the use of flashy lighting and bold color schemes. The small café has a trendy feel and not that of a traditional cramped theater eatery.

The arcade area is also an eye-catching playland for kids of all ages, encouraging people to stay in the facility before or after a film. The designers also incorporated the use of sound to draw attention. Sound monitors, games, musicians and concessions create sound waves conceptually used in three-dimensional expressions of traffic, flows, physical forms and interior features.

In contrast to the busy lobby, the movie theaters themselves are referred to as "black-boxes." They are completely black, to keep the focus on the silver screen, and not distract the viewers.

Design: F/M Associates Inc., Dallas — C. Cal Young, design principal, Lester Cox, project architect; Dean Bowman, David Stewart, Rosanna Ross, Beth Anschuetz, project team
Architect: F/M Associates Inc., Dallas
General Contractor: Austin Commercial, Inc., Dallas
Lighting: SLV, Dallas; F/M Associates Inc., Dallas (neon, fluorescent, custom sconce)
Lighting Consultant: F/M Associates Inc., Dallas
Fixturing: Universal Cinema Services, Dallas; D.P. Industries, Irving, Texas
Flooring: Armstrong, Lancaster, Pa.; Daltile, Dallas; American Marazzi Tile, Sunnyvale, Texas
Furniture: Universal Cinema Services, Dallas
Laminates: Wilsonart, Temple, Texas
Ceiling: Classic Industries Inc., Irving, Texas
Signage: Chandler Signs
Graphics: F/M Associates Inc., Dallas
Audio/Video: SLV, Bill Swigart, Dallas
Wallcoverings: Essex Wallcovering, Pine Brook, N.J.; Melded Wall Carpets
Photography: Charles Smith, Irving, Texas

NRMA RETAIL BRANCH

Sydney, Australia
Geyer Design Pty Ltd., Sydney, Australia

Geyer Design Pty. Ltd.'s objective was to create a new presence, deliver a powerful brand experience and represent future directions for NRMA's retail operation. As the point of orientation for the store, the design team introduced a circular entry that houses organic-shaped customer-service counters, a directory board and a dropped pendant bell-call system. A neutral color palette serves as a backdrop to striking graphic components, and combination hard and soft floor-coverings define circulation routes. From main floor to mezzanine, a white-on-white wall accentuates a vertical connection while glass inserts of laminated rice paper on the balustrade offer a sense of movement and shadow. A weathered-timber platform on the mezzanine level acts as an orientation board and works with suspended department signage, photographic images and colored graphics in the double-height space to reduce the overall volume and ensure NRMA sits comfortably within the modern building envelope.

Design: Geyer Design Pty Ltd., Sydney, Australia — Peter Geyer, managing director; Melinda Huuk, Grant Cheyne, designers; Allan Griffiths, project manager
NRMA Team: Trish Shaw, manager
General Contractor: Wee Datum Shopfitting, Sydney
Lighting Consultant: Barry Webb & Associates, Sydney
Graphics Consultant: Lewis Kahn Stanford, Sydney
Ceiling: BBS Constructions, Sydney
Fixturing: Wee Datum Shopfitters, Sydney
Flooring: Carpet Solutions, Sydney
Laminates: Formica Corp., Sydney
Wallcovering: Dulux, Sydney
Graphics: Flash Graphics, Sydney
Photography: Mark Omeara, Sydney

WELLS FARGO + STARBUCKS PROTOTYPE DESIGN

Multiple Locations
Callison Architecture Inc., Seattle

Today's busy consumer loves the one-stop shop. Wells Fargo and Starbucks decided they would make a great team to help their busy customers. In order to fit together two rather different store images, they called on Callison Architecture, Seattle, to create a seamless flow between them.

Taking from Wells Fargo's stagecoach logo, materials such as wood, leather, limestone and historical props decorate the "third place," the space between home and office. This community gathering place encourages customers to linger and return, while the tenants benefit from each others' peak business hours. Curved walls and contrasting flooring are used to define activity areas. On one side is Starbuck's bold, colorful palette, while on the other, the more reserved Wells Fargo. The design was a play on contrast that seems to effortlessly tie the two together.

Design: Callison Architecture Inc., Seattle — Paula Stafford, design principal; Chris Hamilton, principal-in-charge; Marlo Morgan, project designer; Brian Gowers, Elisa Muller, project architects; Keith Nielson, associate; Bill McKnight, interior designer
Wells Fargo Team: Paul Gore
Starbucks Team: Eric Lagerberg, design project manager; George Murphy, manager
Architect: Callison Architecture Inc., Seattle
General Contractor: Pacific Building Interiors, S. California; CIC Associates, N. California
Design Consultants: Abacus, Seattle
Engineers: AKB Engineers
Lighting Consultant: Candela, Seattle
Fixturing: Village Woodcrafts
Flooring: Associated Imports
Furniture: Martin/Brattrud,, Gardena, Calif.
Wallcovering: Display Products
Props: Propaganda
Centerpiece Clock: Iron Designworks
Photography: Chris Eden, Seattle

WILLOWBEE & KENT TRAVEL CO.

Boston
Retail Design Group, Columbus, Ohio

The focal point of the retail space is a circular cashwrap area and sweeping staircase that leads to the mezzanine level. The store's ceilings, upper walls and the "lantern" behind the transaction area are screens for a constantly changing light, video and special effects show. The 5400-square-foot, two-level store is in a former bank building whose mezzanine was converted to extend retail footage and provide a travel consulting area. The design team made the store polymorphous — using its upper walls, ceiling planes and other surfaces as a canvas and a palette of video, still images and accent lighting to repaint it constantly. A sophisticated control system orchestrates video presentations, preset lighting scenes that sweep across walls and ceilings, accent lighting and sound.

Design: Retail Design Group, Columbus, Ohio — Peter S. Macrae, AIA, consulting principal, Retail Design Group project team
Willowbee & Kent Team: Craig W. Poteet and Julie Poteet
General Contractor: Lee Kennedy Company, Inc., Boston
Design Consultants: Lighting Management Inc., New York City (lighting consultant); HBK Consultants Ltd., Westerville, Ohio (plumbing, mechanical and electrical engineering)
Fixturing: Woodmasters Design & Manufacturing, Bolingbrook, Ill.
Flooring: The Becht Corp., Wilmington, Mass.; Invision Carpet Systems, Dalton, Ga.
Furniture: Rytel & Associates, Montgomery, Ohio
Lighting: Clay Paky/Group One, Farmingdale, N.Y. (lighting/video control system, projectors); Lightolier, Secaucus, N.J.; Progress Lighting, Spartanburg, S.C.; House of Troy, Hyde Park, Vt.; Modular Lighting, Pittsburgh; Mercury Lighting, Fairfield, N.J.; Tivoli Industries Inc., Santa Ana, Calif. (fixtures)
Mannequins/Forms: France Display/Manex, New York City
Graphics: KPI Design, Columbus, Ohio
Signage: KPI Design, Columbus, Ohio
Audio/Video: AEI Music Network, Seattle – John Kershner, systems specialist; Systems Division, Columbus, Ohio (systems design/integration)
Photography: Bruce Martin Photography, Cambridge, Mass.

AUDI SHOWPLACE

Park Avenue, New York City
Grid/3 International Inc., New York City;
JGA, Southfield, Mich.

To draw potential customers into Audi's new Park Avenue showroom (whose location is passed by an estimated 500,000 people each day), the design team had to raise the visibility of the Audi car, adapt Audi's corporate visual standards to the unique setting, and associate the Audi name with the high-tech automotive achievements of the German-engineered brand. The design team decided on a four-ring Audi logo on the exterior of the building, a custom-faceted glass wall inset with fiberoptic lighting that changes colors through the day.

Inside, curving forms inspired by the sleek cars include a beech and stainless steel reception desk. The showroom palette also includes beech column covers, sandblasted glass and custom furnishings that emphasize the German minimalist aesthetic. Stainless steel railings and furniture detailing, polished terrazzo floors and energy-efficient, electronically-programmed lighting emphasize Audi's technical prowess.

Design: Grid/3 International Inc., New York City — Keith Kovar, executive vice president, creative director; Ruth Mellergaard, president, project manager; Jojo Borja, senior draftsperson; Leticia Stella-Serra, junior designer
JGA, Southfield, Mich. — Robert Berlin, executive vice president; Tony Camilletti, vice president of visual communications; Michael Curtis, creative director; Brian Hurtienne, project manager; Mike Opipari, senior draftsperson; Curtis Nemith, draftsperson; Jeri Badernian-Elsie, color and materials specialist; Mike Farris, senior graphic designer
Architect: JGA, Southfield, Mich.
General Contractor: Struction Corp., New York City
Ceiling: Chicago Metallic, Chicago; Kalwall Corp., Manchester, N.Y.
Flooring: D. Magnan, Mt. Vernon, N.Y.; Permagrain, Media, Pa.
Furniture: Design Link, Boston; Davis, High Point, N.C.
Tile: Terra Loha Tile, Troy, Mich.; Boltawall/Thybony, Troy, Mich.
Fabric: Carnegie, New York City
Audio/Video: Audi of America/CORE/Trammell Crow, Troy, Mich.
Photography: Laszlo Regos, Berkeley, Mich.

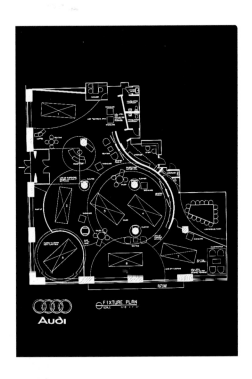

DUCATI SHOWROOM

42nd Street, New York City
Gensler, New York City

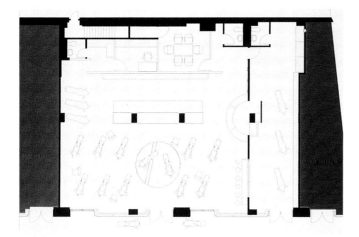

To achieve a stronger worldwide awareness of their brand, Italian motorcycle manufacturer Ducati decided to create a street-level presence in urban centers around the world by giving its potential customers a unique experience. For this showroom prototype in New York City, the design team made use of the perception of the motorcycle as an elegant, highly engineered machine by designing a "jewel box" in which the motorcycle is the jewel. Signature dome lighting fixtures with a series of cuts on top project circular images on the showroom ceiling. A light box display counter features historic items such as motorcycle racing memorabilia, motorcycle clothing and accessories and racing trophies. The back wall of the showroom features enlarged engineering drawings of a Ducati motorcycle. The engineering motif is repeated again on a translucent vinyl surface, visible from both inside and outside, located above the storefront windows and main door.

While the primary function of this retail space is to sell Ducati motorcycles, it also serves as an entertainment venue. On one feature wall running the entire side of the showroom, a photo timeline chronicling motorcycle racing and Ducati's history is displayed. Current racing news and information flash across an LED display integrated into the exhibit. Customers can also visit Club Ducati, relax with a beverage and snack and watch skilled technicians work on motorcycles through a window into the service block.

Design: Gensler, New York City — John Bricker, Mark Morton, design directors; Robert Cataldo, director; Lisa Chu, architect; Gus Hinojosa, architect/designer; Robin Fritzsche, manager; Lisa Van Zandt, Christian Uhl, Elizabeth Bowdle, Kamol Prateepmanowong, graphic designers
General Contractor: F.J. Sciame Co. Inc., New York City
Lighting Consultant: Horton-Lees Lighting Design, New York City
Code Consultant: Charles Rizzo & Associates, New York City
Mechanical/Electrical Consultant: Robert Derector & Associates, New York City
Telecommunications Consultant: Robert Derector & Associates, New York City

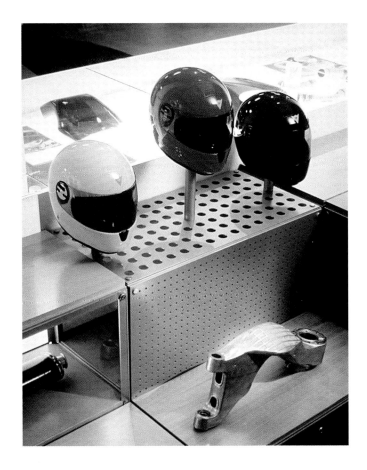

THE STEELCASE WORKLAB

Steelcase Corporate Headquarters, Grand Rapids, Mich.
Lee Stout Inc., New York City

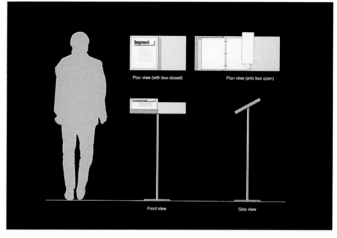

The Steelcase Work Lab was designed to introduce a new family of products, Pathways, and demonstrate how to construct and furnish a total office interior. Customers are greeted in an area furnished "to work," with special lounge chairs on wheels and "smart" tables high enough to allow customers to use their laptop computers while waiting. A counterclockwise traffic flow guides customers through the product line via a series of artful, abstract compositions. Customers entering the "Kit of Parts" are exposed to individual parts and pieces that will later be used to create complete office spaces. The "Work Settings" space features demonstrations of how Pathways products can be used to create total office interiors. Five different settings present various disciplines and material palettes and are identified with projected light and large podiums that display axonometric drawings with bullet copy. The customers' tour ends with a full presentation of the Pathways palette and materials.

Design: Lee Stout Inc., New York City — Jeffrey Osborne, consulting partner; Cam Lorendo, Lynn Campbell, senior designers
Steelcase Team: David Gresham, Peggy Sonnenberg, Carl Leismer
Architect: Lee Stout Inc., New York City
General Contractor: P & D Building, Wyoming, Mich.
Graphic Design Consultants: Donovan & Green, New York City
Lighting: Legion, Brooklyn, N.Y.; Lightolier, Secaucus, N.J.; Luce Plan, New York City; Peerless, Berkeley, Calif.; Poulsen, Miami; Steelcase, Grand Rapids, Mich.; Tech, Chicago
Ceiling: Armstrong, Lancaster, Pa.
Fixturing: Xibitz, Grand Rapids, Mich.
Flooring: Clodan, New York City; Shaw, Dalton, Ga.; Tek-Stil, Haddonfield, N.J.
Access Floors: Steelcase, Grand Rapids, Mich.; Tate, Jessup, Md.
Furniture: Brayton, High Point, N.C.; Metro, Burlingame, Calif.; Steelcase, Grand Rapids, Mich.; Vecta, Grand Prairie, Texas
Laminates: Abet, Cent. Islip, N.Y.; Steelcase, Grand Rapids, Mich.
Wallcovering: Designtex, New York City; Steelcase, Grand Rapids, Mich.
Fabric: Designtex, New York City; Steelcase, Grand Rapids, Mich.
Graphics: Derksen, Orangevale, Calif.; Xibitz, Grand Rapids, Mich.
Signage: Xibitz, Grand Rapids, Mich.
Props: Details, Grand Rapids, Mich.; LSI, New York City
Audio/Video: Steelcase, Grand Rapids, Mich.

COFFEE PEOPLE

Tigard, Ore.
Retail Planning Associates, Columbus, Ohio

I n the increasingly competitive world of caffeine-and-conversation venues, Coffee People wanted to distinguish itself as a distinctly American coffee house, one with 1950s Beat Culture values and 1990s humanist attitudes of tolerance, inclusiveness and individualism. RPA's design combines tongue-in-cheek humor (the tagline, "Good Coffee, No Backtalk" is featured on exterior signage) with civic responsibility, appealing to a young, culturally curious and highly educated consumer.

The store's layout, traffic patterns, floor graphics and suspended-ceiling installations are inspired by Harry Beroia lithographs, chosen for their organic quality and fluid content. The sealed-concrete floor directs traffic flow and inspires reflection with hand-printed organic patterns and words like 'dream' and 'sing' painted on the surface.

Three areas were constructed to meet the daily needs of the coffee consumer: a window bar for hurried "grab 'n go" customers; a living room-type area with overstuffed chairs and side tables that allow afternoon drinkers to get comfortable; and the "rendezvous" zone with its swirling, colored translucent disk suspended from the ceiling. A new logo and identity program support the "corporate" needs of national rollout and the retro-kitschy visual communications and menuboard educate and entertain the customer about bean types, roasts and how coffee flavors are developed. RPA created the Bean-O-Rama identity for whole bean sales, located in the back of the store to draw customers through the store and eliminate traffic jams. Prominent use of gold warms the store palette and provides a toasty and stable counterpoint to the psychedelic suspended ceiling installations.

Design: Retail Planning Associates, Columbus, Ohio — Doug Cheesman, ceo; Mike Bills, senior vice president, account executive; Diane Perduk Rambo, senior vice president, creative director; Jeff McCall, senior vice president, strategy director; Marie Haines, planner, merchandiser; Perry Kotick, lighting designer; Chas Mindigo, visual communications; Diane Perduk Rambo, color/materials; Christian Deuber, photographer
Coffee People Team: Taylor Devine, ceo
Furniture: Loewenstein Inc., Pompano Beach, Fla.; Cipra and Frank, Berkeley, Calif.; Thonet, Statesville, N.C.; Beverly Furniture Mfg. Co., Pico Riveira, Calif.; Berrnis Casual Furniture, Sheboygan, Wis.
Special Finishes: Pratt & Lambert, Marysville, Calif.; Optic Nerve Art Corp, Columbus, Ohio
Laminates: Formica Corp., Cincinnati; Pioneer Plastic Corp., Auburn, Maine; Wilsonart, Temple, Texas
Paint: Sherwin Williams, Cleveland
Fabric: Deepa Textiles, San Francisco
Photography: Courtesy of Retail Planning Associates, Columbus, Ohio

THE NORTH FACE, SUMMIT SHOP

San Leandro, Calif., Triad Manufacturing Inc., St. Louis
Brand + Allen Architects, San Francisco

Wanting to project its image and highly successful philosophy of stylish, technical sophistication within re-sellers' stores, the client restricted its materials palette to metals and plastics, mirroring the construction of their products. The designers incorporated brightly colored products and graphics to play off the monochrome fixture metal. With the integration of the client's refined graphics program, faster customer feedback accelerated the prototyping schedule. The overall concept allows for a family of fixtures to work together in a wide-range display to create a clean, technical identity.

Design: Brand + Allen Architects, San Francisco — Steve Lochte, partner-in-charge; Koonshing Wong, project designer; David Lam, designer
The Summit Shop Team: Mark Shea, senior manager, David Curtis, Summit Shop manager
Architect: Brand + Allen Architects, San Francisco
Fixturing: Triad Manufacturing Inc., St. Louis

GONDOLA FIXTURE

OUTPOST FIXTURE

WATCH STATION AND SUNGLASS HUT INTERNATIONAL

Coconut Grove, Fla.
Michel Dubuc Concept, Montreal

The prototype concept, "Side-by-Side," integrates the two different stores and creates a one-stop shopping destination for fashion accessories. Separate entrances feature similar detailing in facade, signage and window display systems. Both stores share light maple fixture finishes and a silver-coated wall finish while modular fixtures and a cross-through area give both "spaciousness." Contrasting maple and mahogany floor planks are laid out differently in each store and are brought together at the cross-through with an in-laid store logo. Recessed display boxes highlight merchandise and encourage customers to cross between the two. Posters sandwiched between acrylic sheets can be changed and updated to promote different products and/or seasons.

Design: Michel Dubuc Concept, Montreal — Michel Dubuc, architect, partner-in-charge; Fabien Nadeau, architect, senior designer; Kim Zakaib, project coordinator
Sunglass Hut Team: Bill Betts, visual director; Joe Vasbinder, director of construction; Phillipe Hum, project manager
Architect: Michel Dubuc Concept, Montreal
General Contractor: J & B Contractors, Ellicott City, Md.
Lighting: FCA Lighting, Weehawken, N.J.
Fixturing: Genesis Innovations Inc., Fort Collins, Colo.
Flooring: Associated Carpets, New York City
Laminates: Poster Lightboxes — DSA Phototech, Los Angeles
Special Finishes: SHI Graphic Systems, Minneapolis; Zolatone Process Inc., Gloucester, Mass.
Signage: Triangle Signs Services, Baltimore

FERRARI MERCHANDISING UNIT

Avenue De La Republique, Toulon, France
Portland Design Associates, London; CIL International Ltd., London

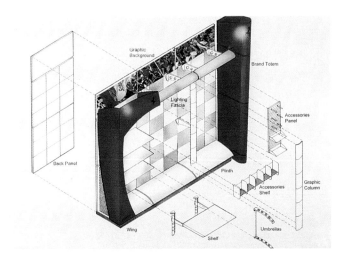

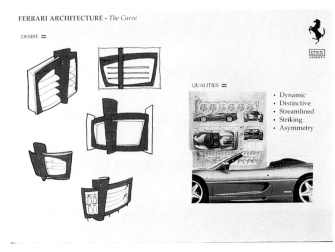

When Nice Man, a major Ferrari licensee, needed a family of merchandising units for its extensive product offering, Ferrari's key criterion was that the units accurately reflect the values and personality of the Ferrari brand. Inspired by the legendary brand and its inherent prestige values, the fixtures were designed to adhere strictly to the Ferrari colors and graphic identity, with red playing a dominant role. Inspired by key Ferrari engineering elements such as the brand wing and totem, the units (metal with satin silver powdercoated finish) were designed to carry specific ranges of Ferrari-endorsed product. The drilled detail on metal structural brackets echoes the Ferrari car steering wheel, and the units were given six coats of red paint to replicate the quality of finish seen on the cars. Strong graphic imagery, illuminated by linear fluorescents within a high-level, semi-elliptical lighting baffle on the merchandising unit, attracts and boosts the desire to purchase.

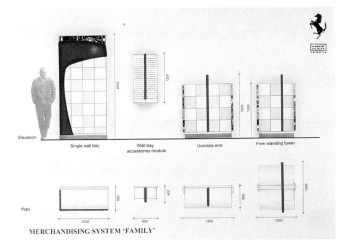

MERCHANDISING SYSTEM 'FAMILY'

Design: Portland Design Associates, London — Stewart Chadick, managing director; Marc Friend, design director
Nice Man Team: Philip Christodoulou
General Contractor: CIL International Ltd., London
Fixturing: CIL International, London
Lighting: Standard Linear Fluorescent, London
Laminates: Abet Laminati, Englewood, N.J.
Graphics: CIL International, London
Signage: CIL International, London
Photography: Courtesy of Nice Man Merchandising, London

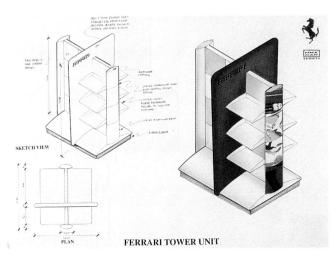

FERRARI TOWER UNIT

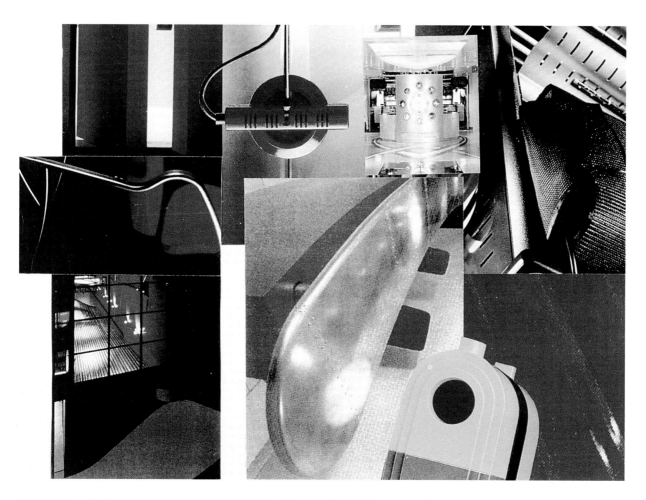

CARHARTT

Imlay, Mich.
Retail Planning Associates, Columbus, Ohio

This shop concept for workwear/accessories is the first in the 100-year-old company's history. Three flexible fixtures were designed to serve the entire inventory, and maintain floor presence for Carhartt through all seasons and sell-throughs. The straightforward fixtures also eliminate the company's erratic presentation in 14 different channels of distribution, and distinguish the workwear line from two new leisure-oriented lines.

The Workhorse fixture features suspension bridge-like cables that create a pulley-like strength while containing the stiff canvas clothing in a manageable space. The Accessories Fixture is designed with peg hooks and hang bars for displaying varying quantities of items and provides a built-in door for access to storage space inside. The Wall System is designed for both visual impact and extra storage. Brown duck Carhartt coats are stored in face-out fashion above the usable racks to broadcast the line in its most recognizable form at the sightline generally occupied by store department signage.

Design: Retail Planning Associates, Columbus, Ohio — Doug Cheesman, ceo; Diane Perduk Rambo, creative director; Jeff McCall, strategy director; Aaron Spiess, account executive; Jennifer Barrett, senior retail strategist; Jason Hudson, retail strategist; Laura Evans, project director; Therese McCann, merchandiser; Michael Torok, environmental designer; David Denniston, graphic designer
Carhartt Team: Mike L. Majsack, market manager; Jane Niemi, product development
Fixturing: Matrix Fixtures, Hastings on the Hudson, N.Y.

GNC LIVE WELL

Burlington Mall, Burlington, Mass.
Robert Edson Swain Inc., Seattle

General Nutrition Centers decided to align their nutritional supplement retailing with the contemporary spirit of living well. The project not only sought to capture this spirit but also to project a call to reclaim authority over our health. Natural birch and cherry veneers, accented with steel and glass, create a warm, inviting environment, and energetic combinations of steel, glass and graphic art infuse the room with grace, power and elegance. The glowing tea ball represents evolving attitudes toward health and the contrast between raw pine shelving and finished ceiling panels represents an instinctive embrace of the natural.

Design: Robert Edson Swain Inc., Seattle — Robert Edson Swain, Bruce Owensby, Clive Pohl, Colin Brandt, design team
GNC Team: Bill Watts, Greg Horn, Karla Willman, Peter Ferri
Architect: Robert Edson Swain Inc., Seattle
General Contractor: Biltmore Construction Co., Burlington, Mass.
Lighting: Juno Lighting, Des Plaines, Ill.
Ceiling: USG Interiors Inc., Chicago
Fixturing: Triad Manufacturing Co., St. Louis
Flooring: Colucci Tile, Pittsburgh
Furniture: Pottery Barn, New York City
Fabric: Broadway National Sign Co., New York City
Graphics: Big Apple Sign Co., New York City

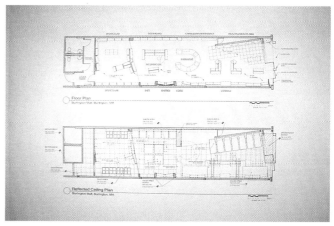

THE NORTH FACE, SUMMIT SHOP

San Leandro, Calif., Triad Manufacturing Inc., St. Louis
Brand + Allen Architects, San Francisco

When North Face was developing a new fixture program for its vendor shops, they wanted to use materials not currently being used by their competition. So they decided to use materials borrowed from their own line of mountain climbing gear and outdoor apparel products. Brushed aluminum is commonly used in fabrication of their equipment. The blue in the frosted glass is a direct derivative of the blue in clamps used as locking devices and is symbolic of the blue sky as a natural element. Wire cable, especially important to any mountain climber, is used on the sides of displays throughout the shop. The fixtures, which range from low to high, aisle to wall and floor to center within the shop, provide flexibility and movement while conveying a concise brand message with minimal merchandise presentation.

Design: The North Face, San Leandro, Calif. — Sandy Walt, David Curtis
Brand + Allen Architects, San Francisco — Steve Lochte, partner-in-charge;
Koonshing Wong, project designer
Architect: Brand + Allen Architects, San Francisco
Fixturing: Triad Manufacturing Inc., St. Louis
Props: ISP Membership, Pittsburgh

The North Face

Backpacks

When your life depends on the performance of your gear, you choose The North Face.

ydroSeal

PACIFIC SCIENCE CENTER, BOEING IMAX THEATER

Seattle
Callison Architecture Inc., Seattle

Pacific Science Theater wanted to maintain its image and enhance user-friendliness by promoting simple choice-making and activity navigation for its visitors. Callison Architecture, recognizing the equity in the theater's architectural identity, including its IMAX Theater, developed a "big door" and trailblazer sign concept. A large pylon sign decorated using IMAX film stock with ScotchPrint Laser Imagery perforations serves as the "big door" for the IMAX. Exhibit and activity information is presented by category of interest, keyed to numbered graphics or theater/restaurant names and activities. The trailblazer signs occur often, inside and outside, to provide wayfinding direction. The wedges feature display cases for event announcement and link visually to the "big door" wedges.

Design: Callison Architecture Inc., Seattle — Robert Tindall AIA, coo; Douglas Stelling, design director; Kevin Mequet, manager-in-charge; Michael Riggs, lead designer, Ron Singler, designer
Pacific Science Center Team: Carole Grisham, associate director; Kay Wilson, planning and finance coordinator; Diane Carlson, director of visitor services and public programs; David Taylor, director of science and exhibits
General Contractor: SignTech, Mountlake Terrace, Wash.
Lighting Consultants: Candela, Seattle; Skilling Ward Magnusson Barkshire, Seattle
Lighting: Nelson Electric, Seattle
Signage: Electronic & Video Display, Bellevue, Wash.
Photography: Chris Eden, Seattle

DOMINO'S PIZZA

Ann Arbor, Mich.
Addison, New York City

Frequent and longstanding customers of Domino's Pizza might know their local delivery phone number, but most can't tell you the location or the look of the store itself. The clients, therefore, charged the design team to attract a new generation of consumers by providing a store with a more inviting look and reminding everyone of the quality of fresh products their pizzas offer. The bright storefront pulls the customer in to a warm palette that makes the service area more inviting and consumer focused. The design scheme and unique counter displays capture consumer attention and deliver the motto, "number one name in pizza delivery," to an expanded clientele in a new way.

Design: Addison, New York City — Phil Seefeld, partner-in-charge; David Takbuchi, design director; Kraig Kessel, creative director; Moe Suleiman, designer; John Creson, senior designer, Robin Kumabe, color and materials Domino's Team: Tom Monaghan, president; Cheryl Bachelder, executive vice president of marketing; Gary Staub, marketing
Architect: D&E Architects, Dallas
Graphics Consultant: Ross Roy Communications, Ann Arbor, Mich.
Signage: Acme-Wiley, Elk Grove Village, Ill.; Capitol Sign

LONGWOOD GALLERIA FOOD COURT

Longwood Galleria, Boston
Prellwitz/Chilinski Associates Inc., Cambridge, Mass.

The client wanted to give the space a new, revitalized energy that captures the spirit of shopping and dining, and charged the design team to seek out the attention of those who use the space as a short-cut between the nearby transit station and surrounding hospitals. Concentrating first on areas of highest visibility, the team designed new entry portals, tower signage, directories and graphic murals. New tenant signage guidelines encourage individual identity and unique icon forms highlight each tenant. The Food Court, given a limited palette of signage and graphic finishes, employs bold color to envelope the public space and uses abstract shapes to animate the environment. Canopies, marquees, blade signs, awnings and dimensional murals are orchestrated to produce a dramatic effect.

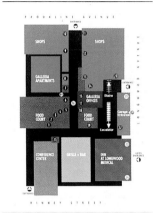

Design: Prellwitz/Chilinski Associates Inc., Cambridge, Mass. — David Chilinski, AIA, principal-in-charge; Mark Connor, AIA, project architect; Jane Sullivan, project designer; Susan Greco, interior designer; Chris Brown, Lisa Mishurda, team members
General Contractor: Alterisio Construction, Burlington, Mass.
Graphic Design Consultants: Guarino Design Group, Cambridge, Mass.
Lighting: Lightolier, Fall River, Mass.; Halo, Elk Grove Village, Ill.
Furniture: Ironworks Ltd., Waterloo, Ont.
Tile: Buchtal, Alpharetta, Ga.; Ceramica Vogue, Key Biscayne, Fla.; Ceramiche Caesar, Italy
Laminates: Formica Corp., Cincinnati; Nevamar Corp., Odenton, Md.
Paint: Benjamin Moore, Montvale, N.J.
Signage: Architectural Graphic Signs, Waltham, Mass.; General Sign Company, Boston; Nordquist Sign Company, Minn.; SRP Signs, Waltham, Mass.

730 N. MICHIGAN AVE.

Chicago
Elkus/Manfredi Architects Ltd., Boston

Totaling approximately 230,000 square feet, the 730 North Michigan Avenue block of Chicago's Magnificent Mile includes three stories of retail and restaurant space. To create street-oriented stores while maintaining their distinct identities and branding, the designer allowed each tenant, including Tiffany & Company, Pottery Barn, Banana Republic, Polo Ralph Lauren and Comp USA, to determine floor-to-floor heights, column spacing and exterior facade treatments. Indiana limestone, Kasota stone, precast concrete, cast-stone, GFRC and steel transformed the one-of-a-kind flagship stores into separate "buildings" for the passing or directed consumer.

Design: Elkus/Manfredi Architects Ltd., Boston — Howard Elkus FAIA, RIBA, principal-in-charge; Robert Koup, project manager; Jeffrey Sakowitz, project architect; William Bunting, James Cyr, Nancy Proudfit, James Solverson, Yossi Zinger, Will Gerstmeyer, design team
Client Design Team: Thomas J. Klutznick Company, Chicago — Thomas Klutznick, Karen Klutznick, Daniel Klutznick, Steven Rudolph, Al Drogosz, John Gagnier Himmel and Company Inc., Boston — Kenneth Himmel
General Contractor: W.E. O'Neil Construction Co., Chicago
Structural Engineer: John A. Martin & Associates, Los Angeles
Design Architects: Pottery Barn — Backen Arrigoni & Ross Inc., San Francisco; Polo Ralph Lauren — James Harb Architects P.C., New York City (townhouse); Polo/Ralph Lauren Store Design, Peter Marino Architect, Naomi Leff and Associates Inc. (mansion); Tiffany & Co. — Elkus/Manfredi with Tiffany & Co. in-house design team; Banana Republic — Elkus/Manfredi with Banana Republic in-house design team; CompUSA — Elkus/Manfredi
Photography: Bob Shimer, Hedrich Blessing Photography, Chicago

THE CHAINERY

The Stratosphere, Las Vegas
Miroglio Architecture + Design, Oakland, Calif.

The storefront was designed as an overall expression of a jewelry store that sells gold creations almost exclusively by weight. To express and symbolize that uniqueness, the entrance facade and its components form a giant weighing scale highlighted with low-voltage floodlights. Two custom cabinets finished in bird's eye maple, positioned on either side of the storefront, provide the base imagery. The central feature, a suspended, elaborately detailed dish holding an assortment of gold chains, is extended to the interior, via pulley and cable, to a giant suspended gold ingot.

Design: Miroglio Architecture + Design, Oakland, Calif. — Joel Miroglio, design; Farhat Daud, design assistant
Chainery Team: Ezra Bekhor, Mira Jurasek
Architect: Miroglio Architecture + Design, Oakland, Calif.
General Contractor: Zeller Enterprises, Henderson, Nev.
Ceiling: USG Interiors, Chicago
Fixturing: Specialties in Wood, Las Vegas
Flooring: A.R. Associates, Corte Madera, Calif.
Laminates: Formica Corp., Cincinnati
Signage: Chapparal Sign Company, Las Vegas

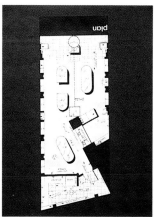

DISNEY'S WORLDPORT

**The Pointe Shopping Center, Orlando,
Walt Disney Attractions Inc., Lake Buena Vista, Fla.**

Asked to command attention and provide a sense of arrival for Disney's WorldPort in Orlando's newly developed outdoor mall, the designers considered their client's internationally recognizable animated characters as the best way to do so. Rich colors and an 80-ft.-long Art Deco-inspired bas relief sign displaying a train of Disney characters welcomes every-one aboard to visit the Walt Disney World Resort. Additional bas relief, emphasized with appropriate materials and lighting, show other theme park locations including Disney-MGM Studios, Epcot, Magic Kingdom Park and Animal Kingdom.

Design: Walt Disney Attractions Inc., Lake Buena Vista, Fla. — Johnnie P. Rush III, director of store planning; Tony Mancini, vice president of retail store development; Kevin Callahan, visual merchandising manager; Stefan Helwig, Mike Montague, Walt Disney Imagineering
Architect: Jon Greenberg & Associates Inc., Southfield, Mich.
General Contractor: TDS Construction, Bradenton, Fla.
Design Consultants: Ibarra Collaborative Inc., Orlando; Pamela Temples Interiors, Orlando
Lighting: Illuminart, Ypsilanti, Mich.
Fixturing: Fetzer's, Salt Lake City; Westco, New York City
Signage: Don Bell Industries, Port Orange, Fla.
Mannequins/Forms: Greneker, Los Angeles
Props: Retail Store Development Production, Orlando; Ace Design, Bristol, Pa.

RAVENNA GARDENS

University Village, Seattle
The Retail Group, Seattle

This garden-inspired gift store concept employs the look of a large greenhouse to appeal to expert as well as novice gardeners. Exterior trellises serve as merchandisers for plants and products, while individual vignettes with live plants and non-plant products help attract even the curious non-gardeners and add to the integration of the concept, "wisdom of soil and soul."

Design: The Retail Group, Seattle — J'Amy Owens, president, creative director; Christopher Gunter, AIA, ceo; Linda Adams, project manager; Greg Arhart, co-creative director; Kim Myran, store planner; Shannon McCafferty, graphic designer
General Contractor: Haringa Corporation, Seattle
Lighting: Lightolier, Secaucus, N.J
Fixturing: Cascade Fixture Company, Puyallup, Wash.
Flooring: CSM, Woodinville, Wash.
Signage: Dwinnell's, Seattle

INDEX OF DESIGN FIRMS

For more information on visual merchandising and store design, subscribe to:

Books on visual merchandising and store design available from ST Publications:

Budget Guide to Retail Store Planning & Design
In-Store Signage & Graphics: Connecting With Your Customer
Stores and Retail Spaces 1
Visual Merchandising 1
Visual Merchandising 2
Visual Merchandising and Store Design Workbook

To subscribe, order books or to request a complete catalog of related books and magazines,
please contact:

ST Publications, Inc.
407 Gilbert Avenue
Cincinnati, Ohio 45202

Telephone 1-800-421-1321 or 513-421-2050
Fax 513-421-5144 or 513-421-6110
E-mail: books@stpubs.com
Web sites: www.visualstore.com and www.stpubs.com